FOR ORGANS, PIANOS & ELECTRONIC KEYBOARDS

E·Z PLAY® TODAY

294

E.P.L.-CPL

Old-Fashioned Love Songs

D1132766

ISBN 0-7935-9314-X

HAL•LEONARD®
CORPORATION

7777 W. BLUEMOUND RD. P.O. BOX 13819 MILWAUKEE, WI 53213

E-Z PLAY ® TODAY Music Notation © 1975 by HAL LEONARD CORPORATION

Visit Hal Leonard Online at
www.halleonard.com

2

Old-Fashioned Love Songs

C O N T E N T S

Always

Registration 2
Rhythm: Waltz

Words and Music by
Irving Berlin

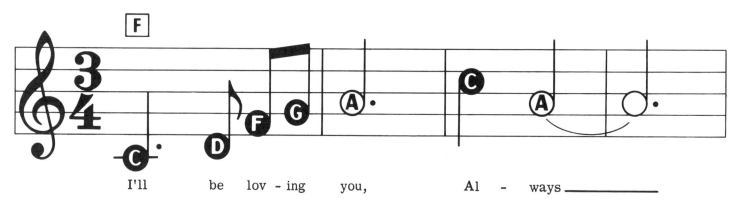

I'll be lov - ing you, Al - ways _____

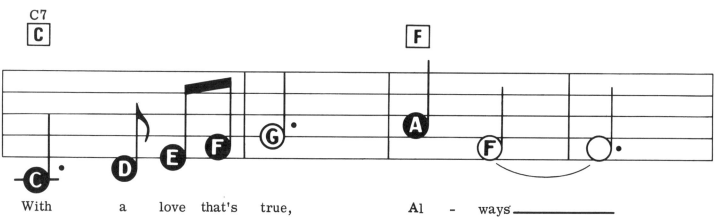

With a love that's true, Al - ways _____

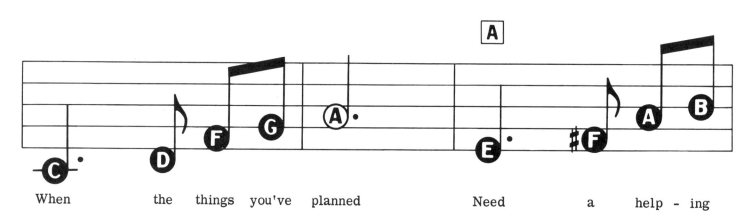

When the things you've planned Need a help - ing

hand, I will un - der - stand,

5

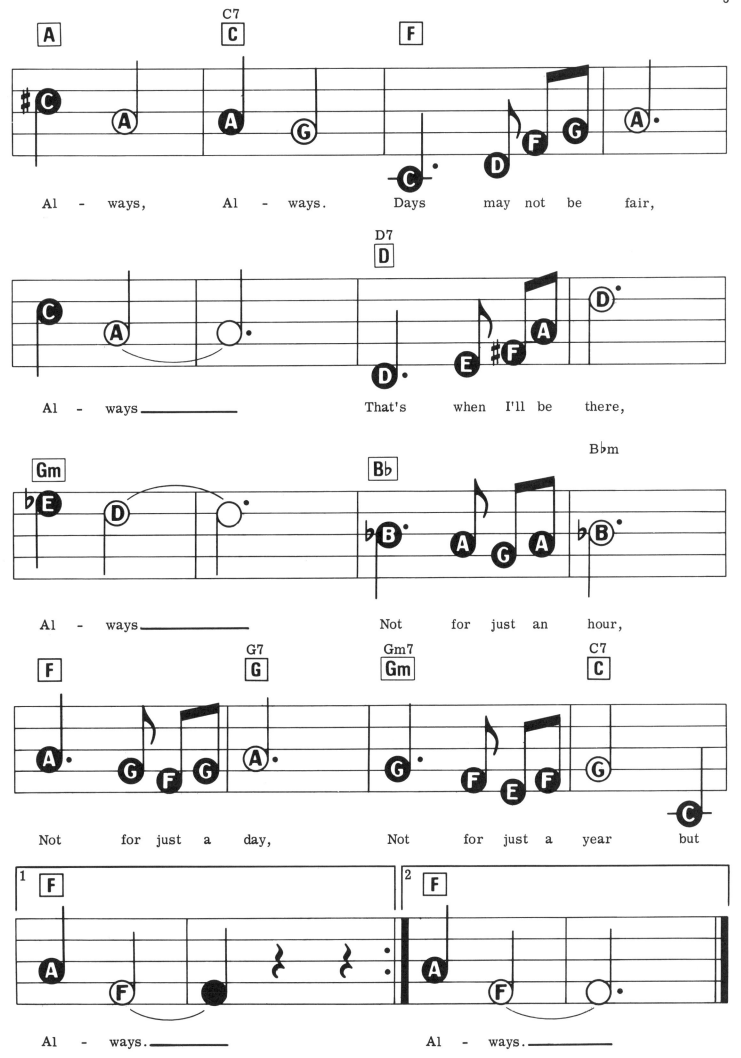

Anniversary Song
from the Columbia Picture THE JOLSON STORY

By Al Jolson
and Saul Chaplin

Registration 6
Rhythm: Waltz

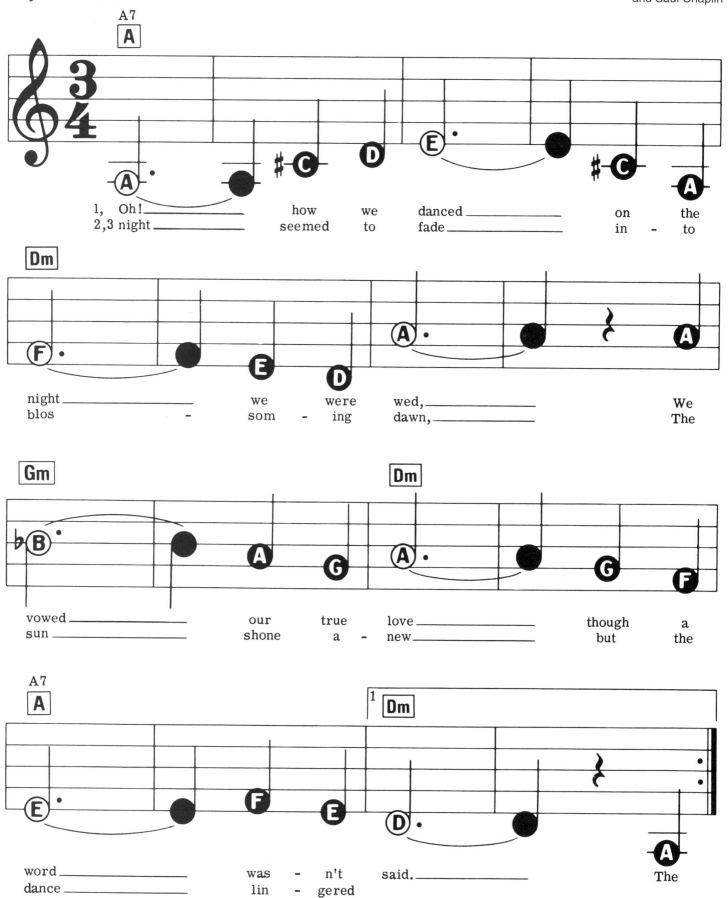

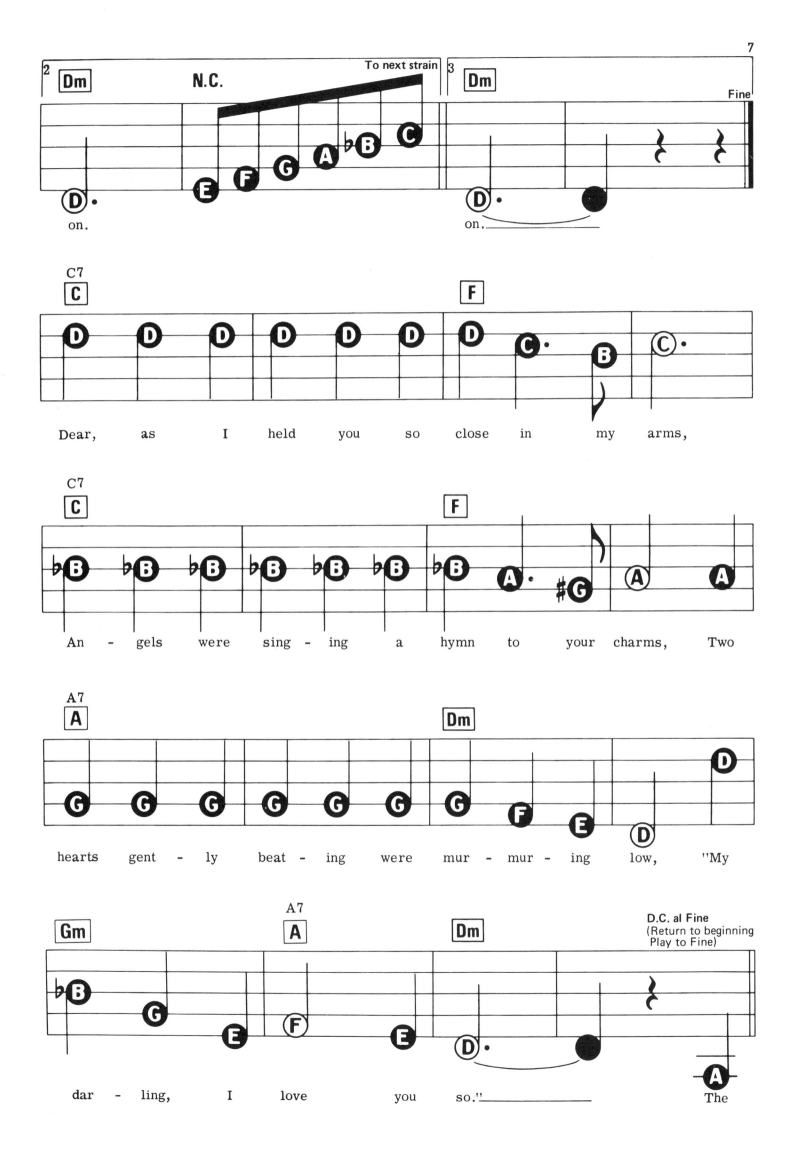

The Anniversary Waltz

Registration 3
Rhythm: Waltz

Words and Music by Al Dubin
and Dave Franklin

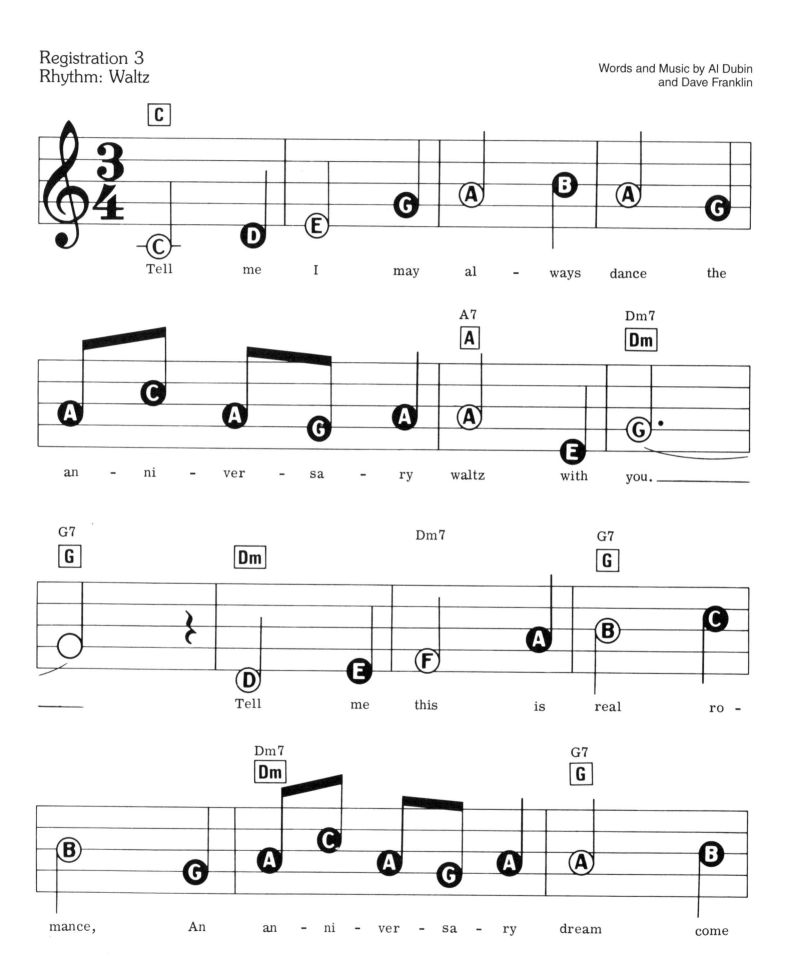

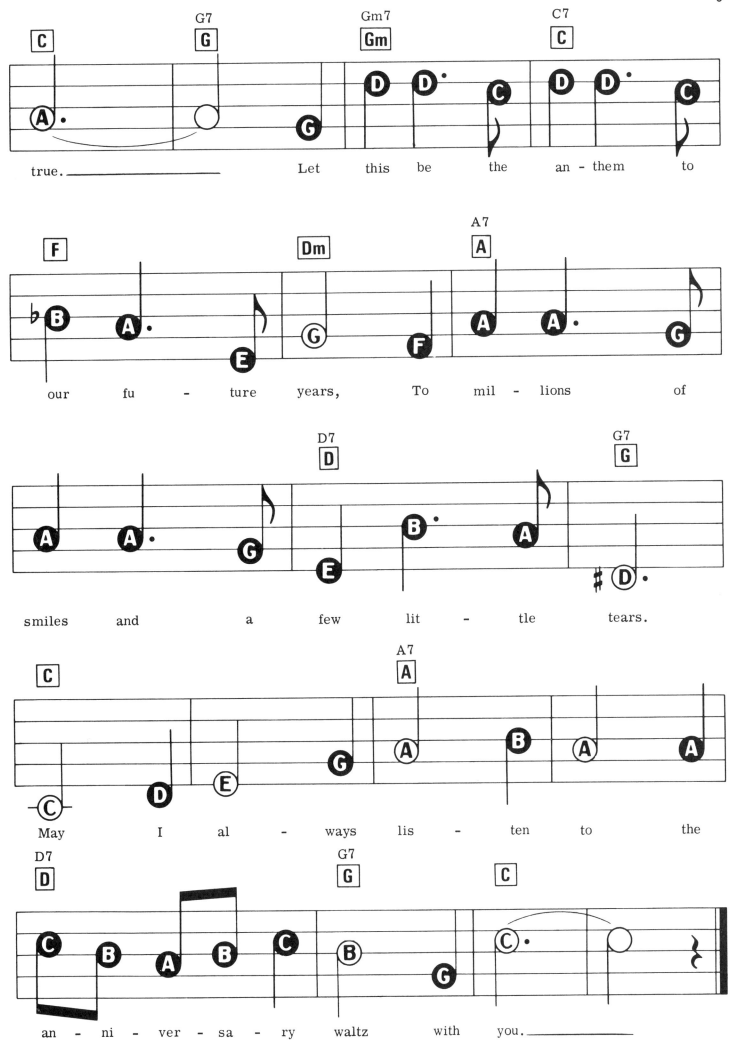

Because

Registration 6
Rhythm: Fox Trot

Words by Edward Teschemacher
Music by Guy D'Hardelot

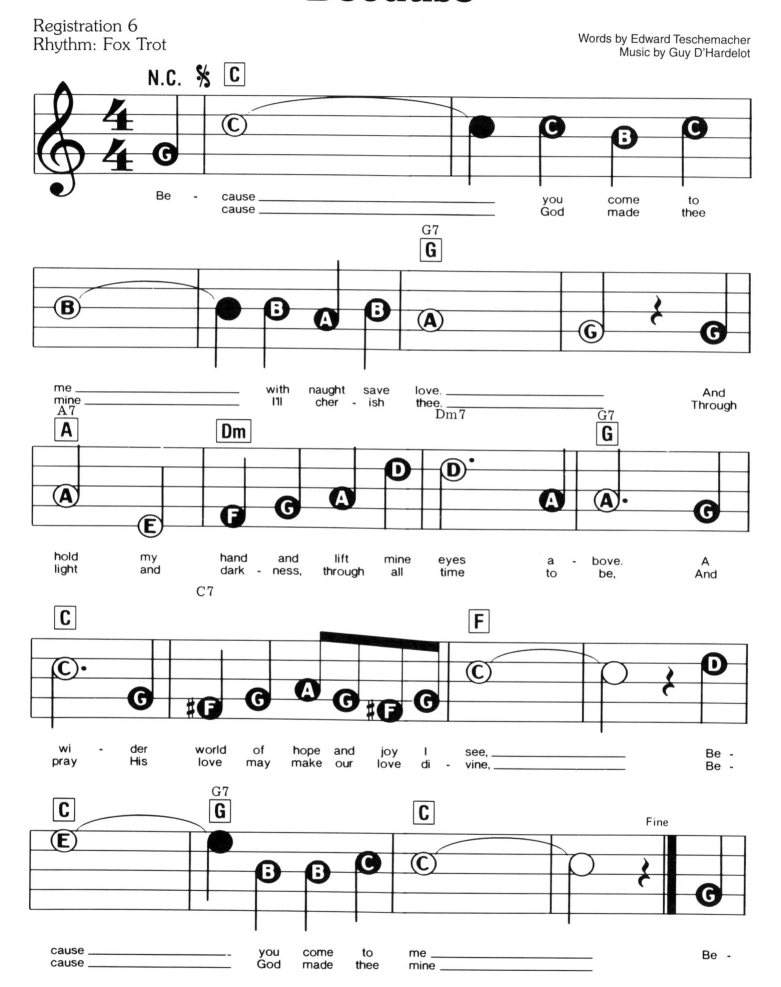

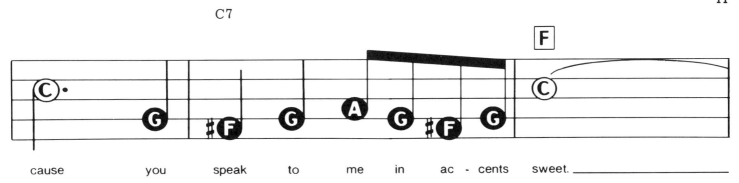

cause   you   speak   to   me   in   ac - cents   sweet. _____

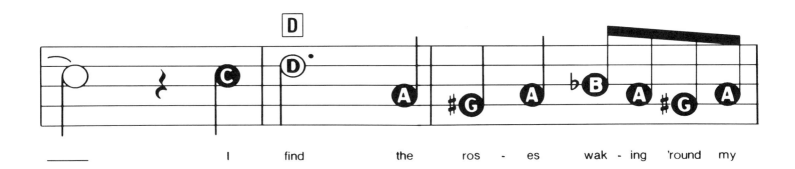

_____   I   find   the   ros - es   wak - ing   'round   my

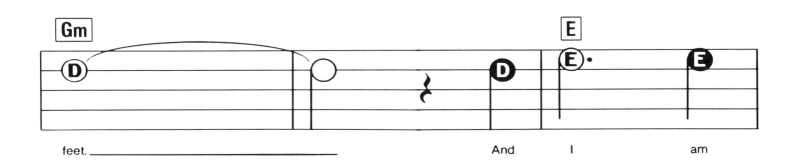

feet. _____   And   I   am

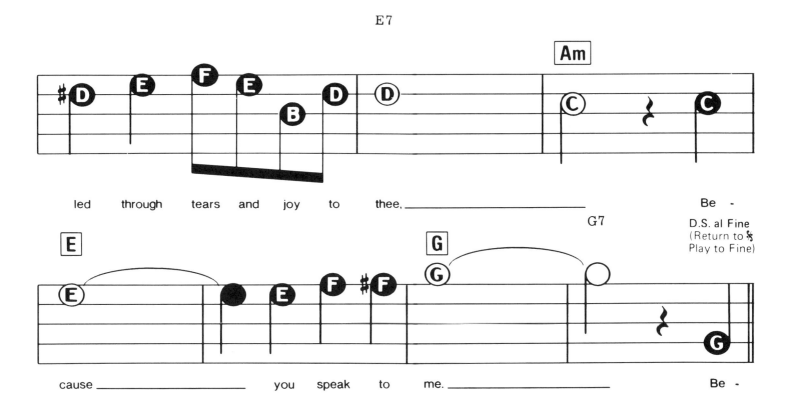

led   through   tears   and   joy   to   thee, _____   Be -

D.S. al Fine
(Return to 𝄋
Play to Fine)

cause _____   you   speak   to   me. _____   Be -

By the Light of the Silvery Moon

Registration 2
Rhythm: Fox Trot or Swing

Lyric by Ed Madden
Music by Gus Edwards

Candy

Registration 4
Rhythm: Fox Trot or Swing

Words and Music by Mack David,
Joan Whitney and Alex Kramer

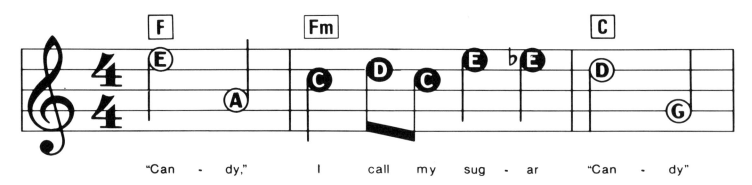

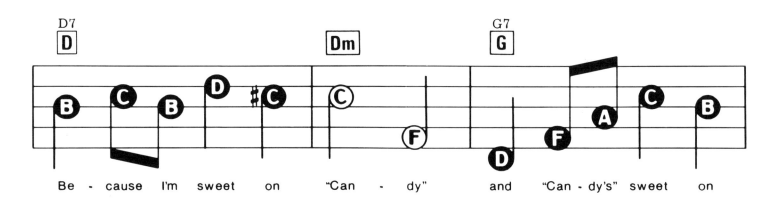

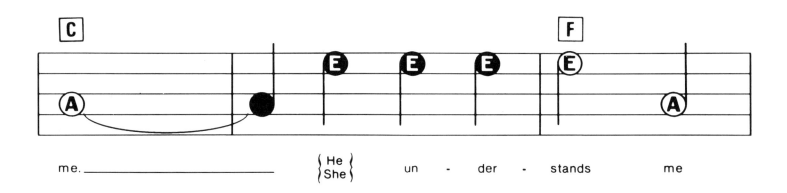

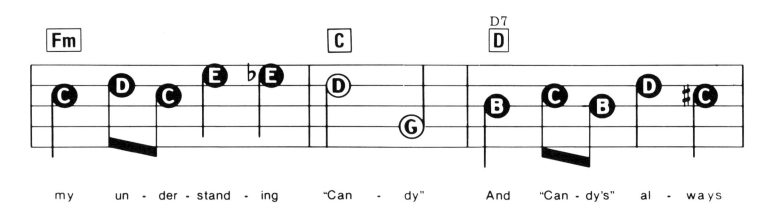

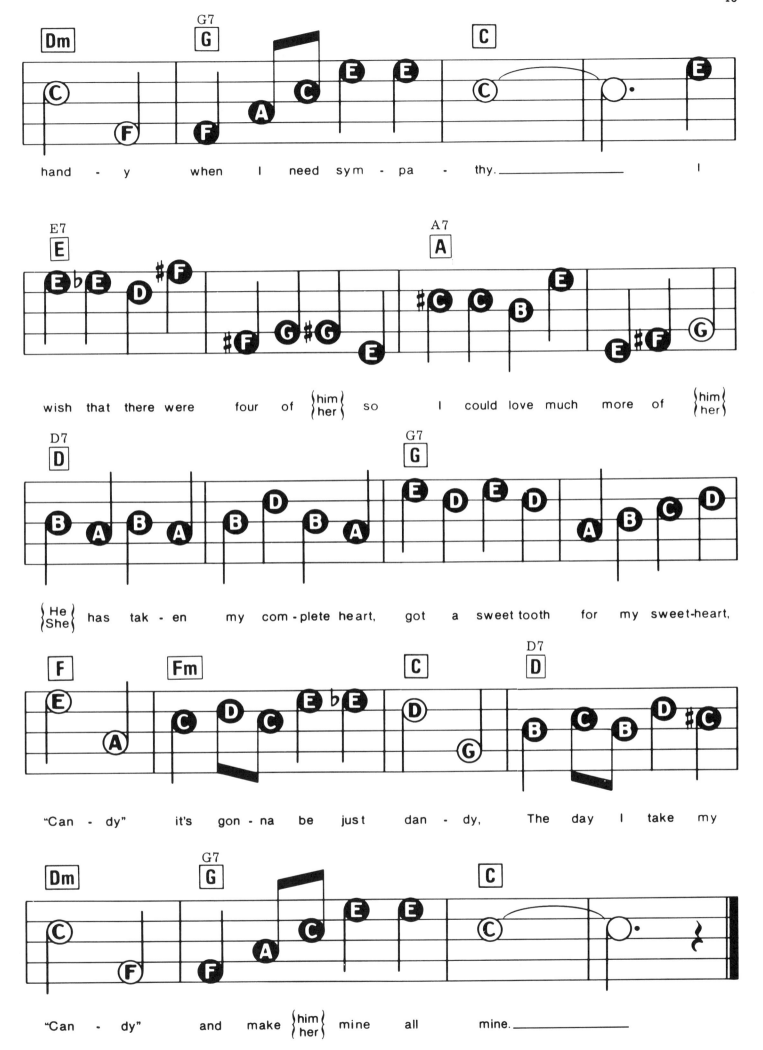

Cuddle Up a Little Closer, Lovey Mine

Registration 3
Rhythm: Swing

Words by Otto Harbach
Music by Karl Hoschna

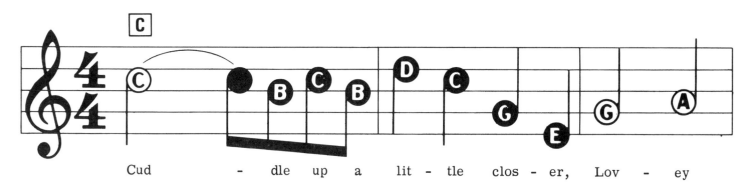

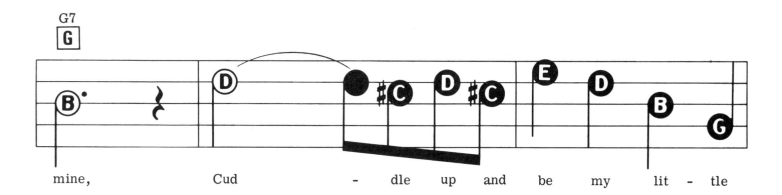

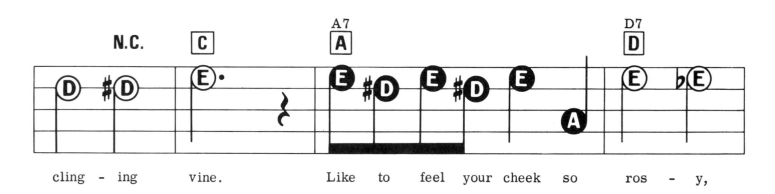

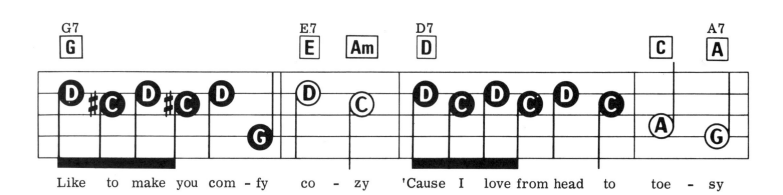

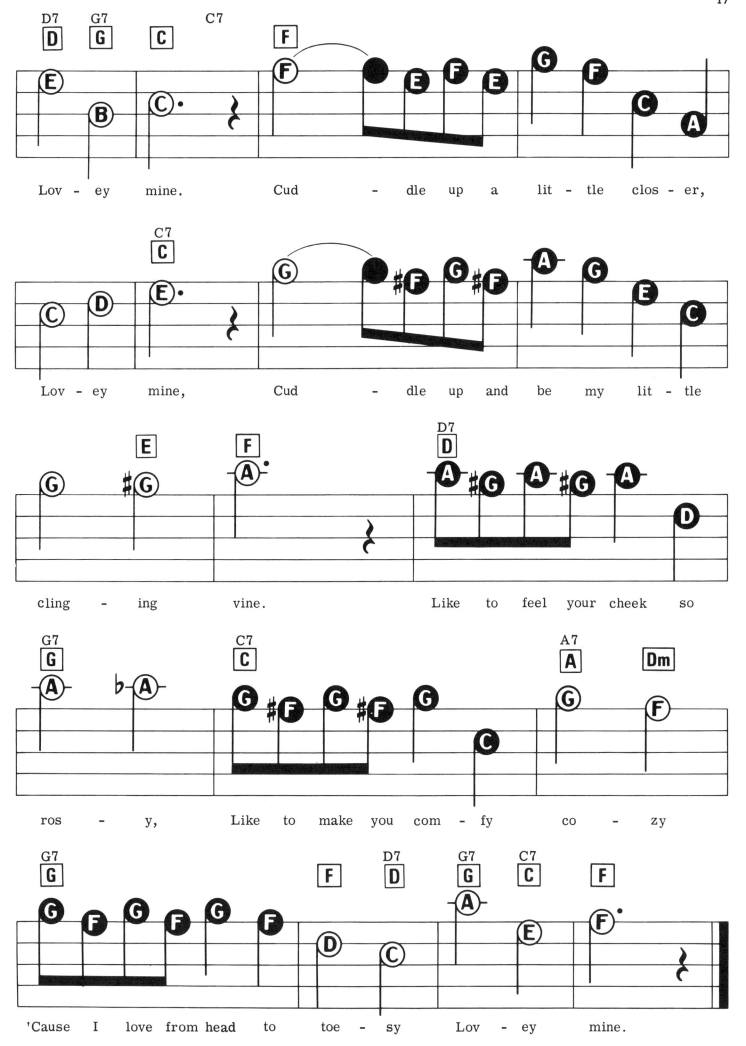

Danke Schoen

Registration 9
Rhythm: Swing

Lyrics by Kurt Schwabach and Milt Gabler
Music by Bert Kaempfert

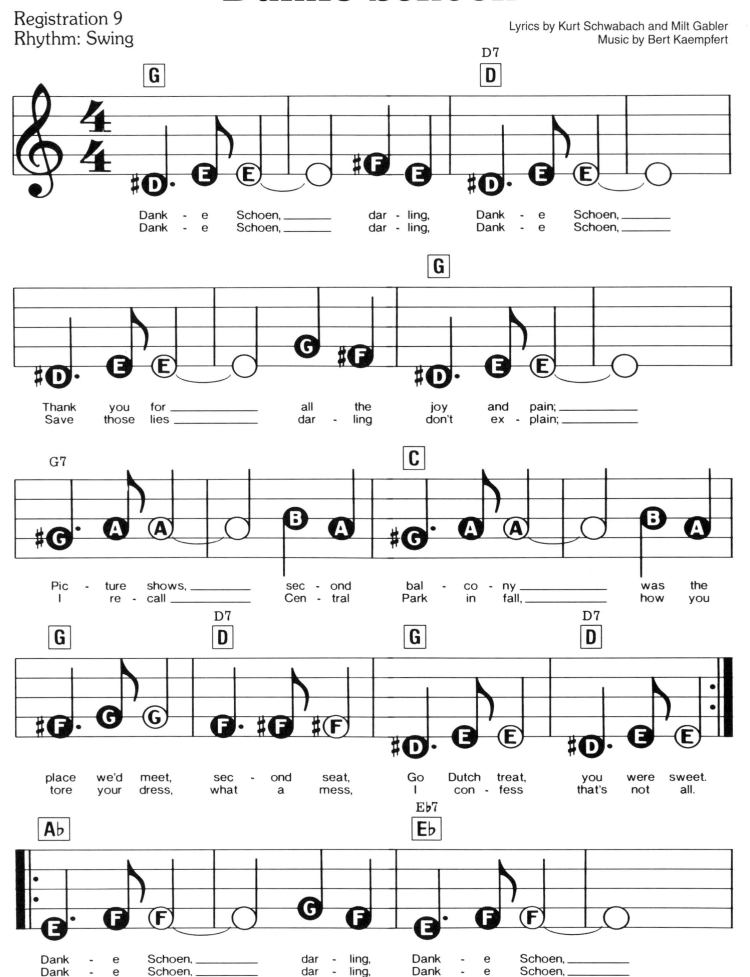

Darling, Je Vous Aime Beaucoup

from LOVE AND HISSES

Registration 3
Rhythm: Fox Trot or Swing

Words and Music by
Anna Sosenko

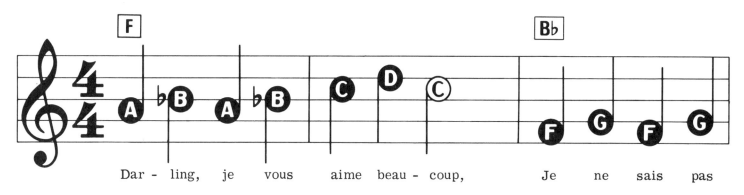

Dar - ling, je vous aime beau - coup, Je ne sais pas

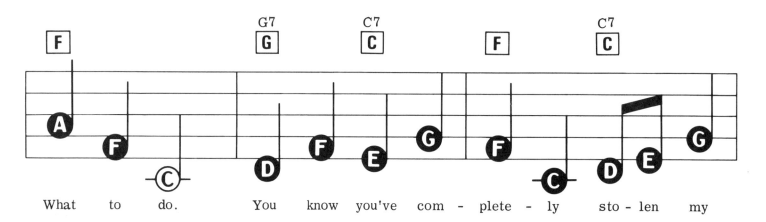

What to do. You know you've com - plete - ly sto - len my

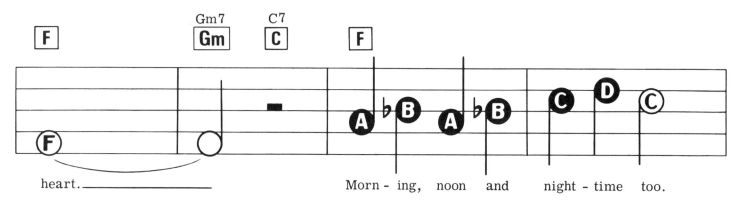

heart. ____ Morn - ing, noon and night - time too.

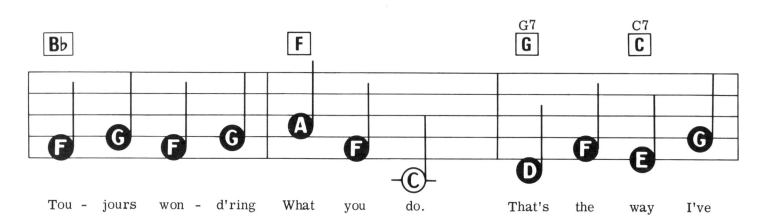

Tou - jours won - d'ring What you do. That's the way I've

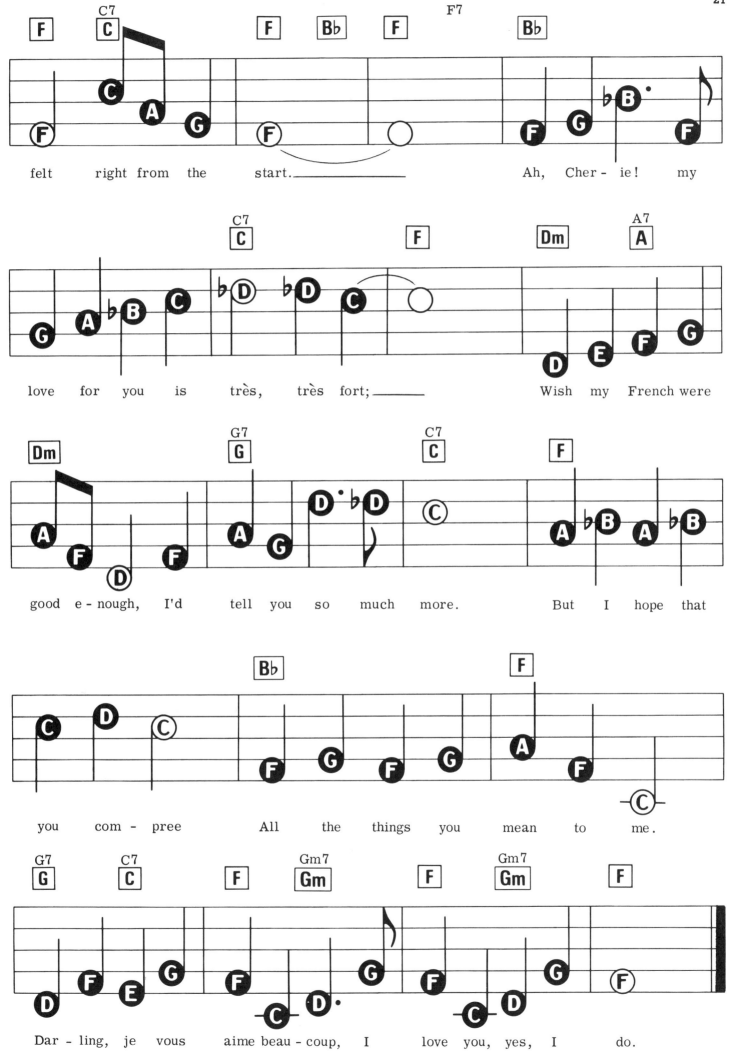

Down by the Old Mill Stream

Registration 3
Rhythm: Waltz

Words and Music by
Tell Taylor

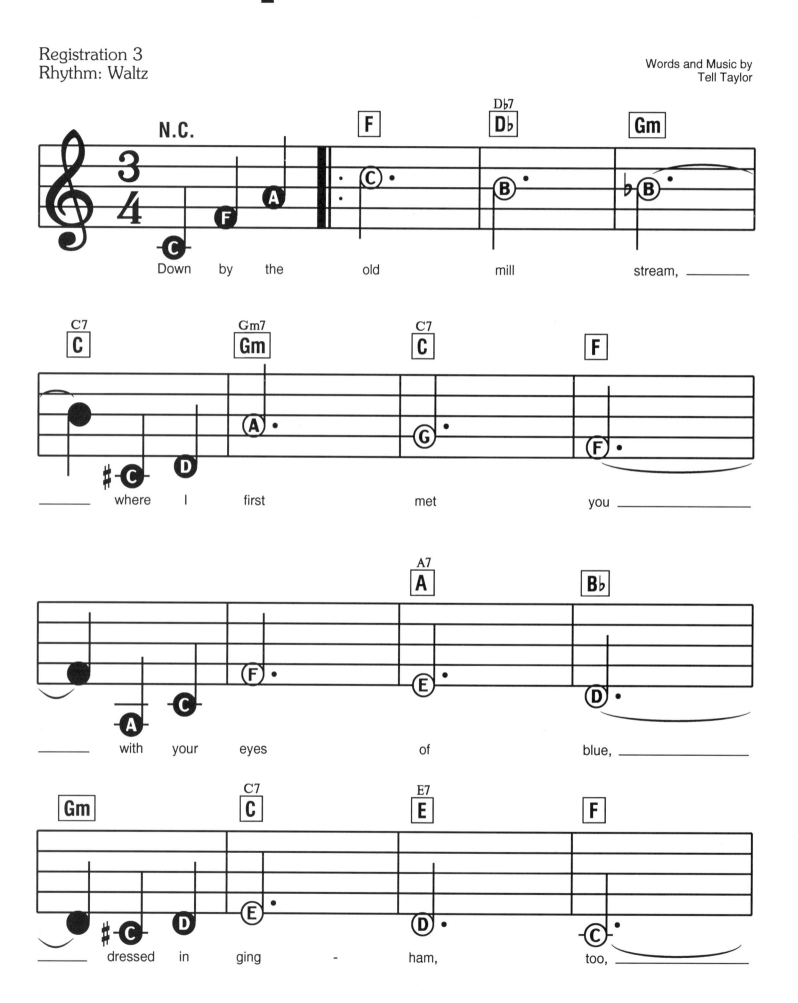

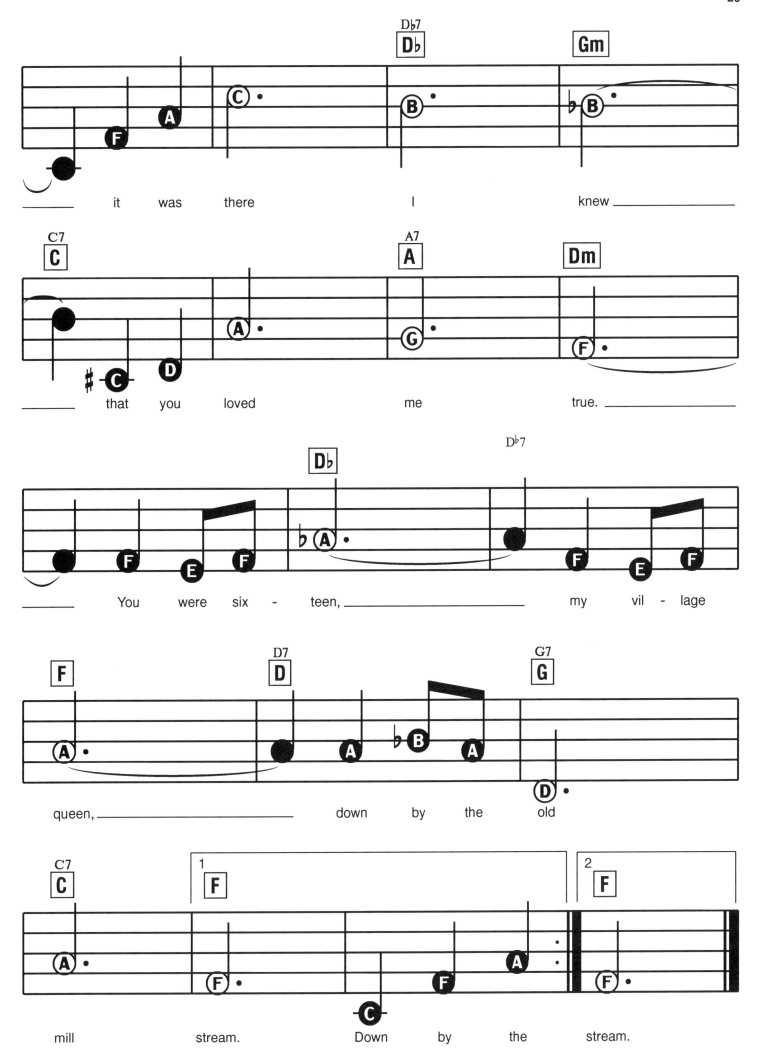

Dream a Little Dream of Me

Registration 4
Rhythm: Ballad or Fox Trot

Words by Gus Kahn
Music by Wilbur Schwandt and Fabian Andree

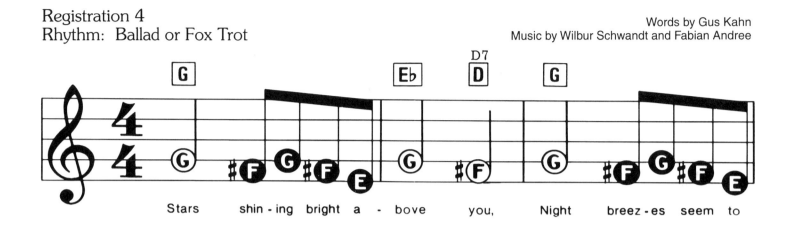

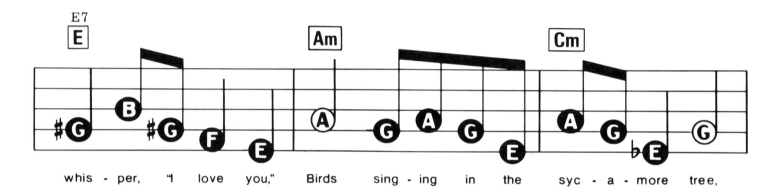

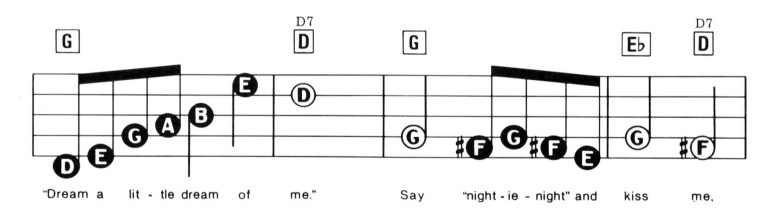

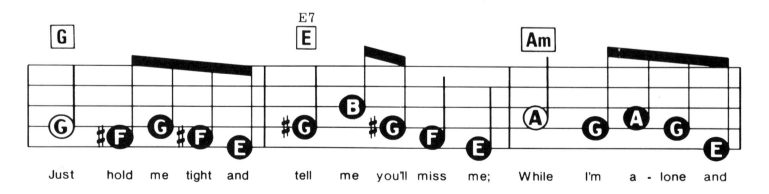

25

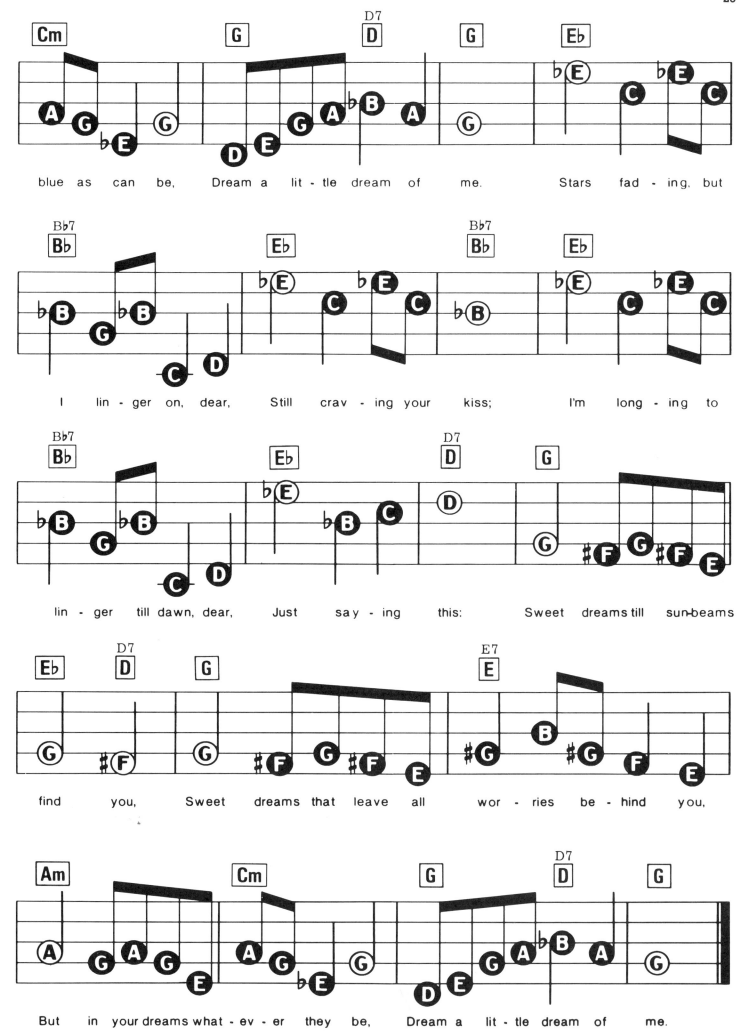

East of the Sun
(And West of the Moon)

Registration 9
Rhythm: Swing or Jazz

Words and Music by
Brooks Bowman

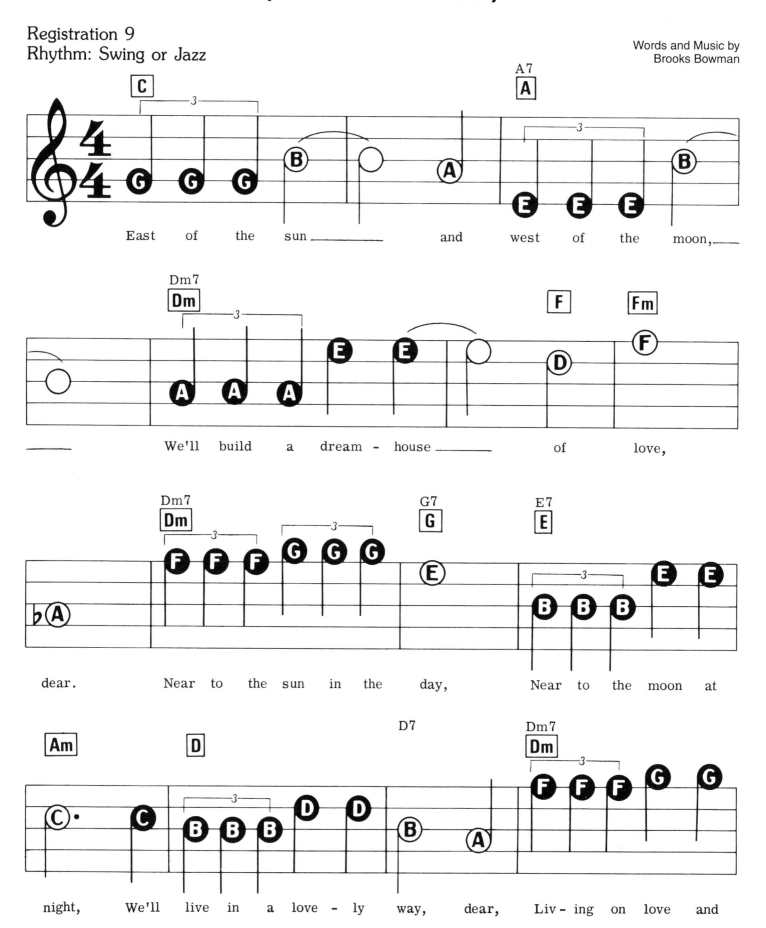

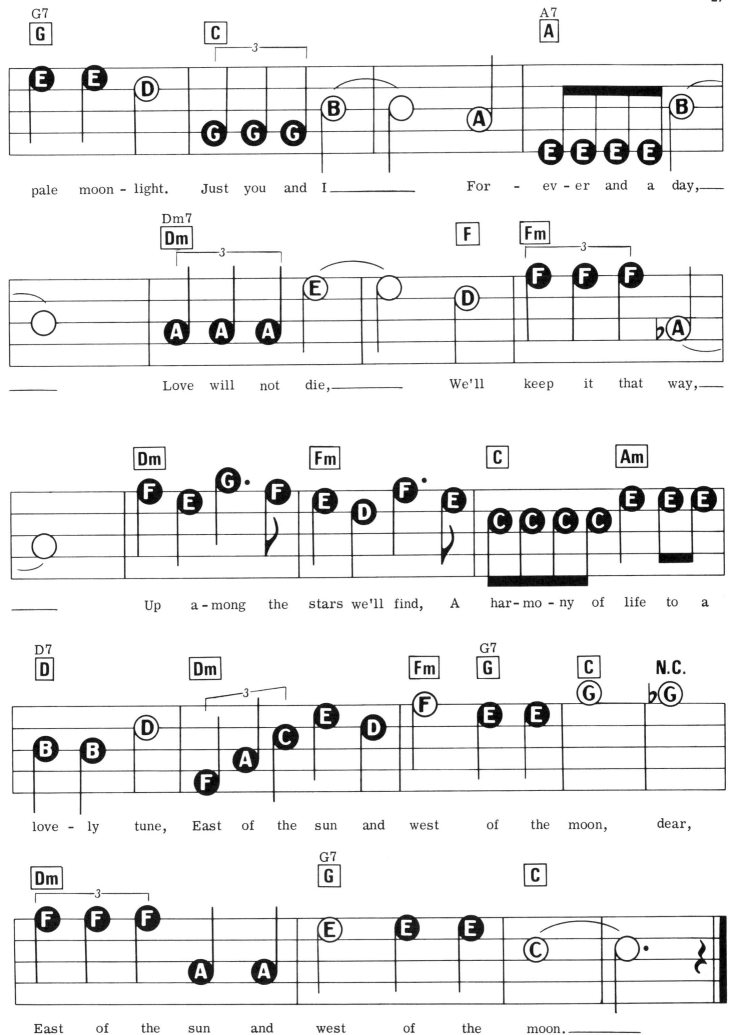

The Folks Who Live on the Hill

from HIGH, WIDE AND HANDSOME

Registration 3
Rhythm: Fox Trot or Swing

Lyrics by Oscar Hammerstein II
Music by Jerome Kern

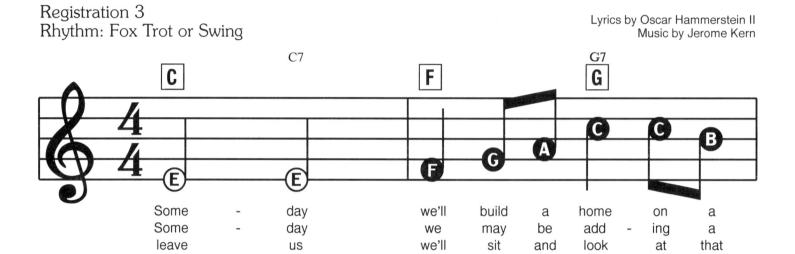

Some - day we'll build a home on a
Some - day we may be add - ing a
leave us we'll sit and look at that

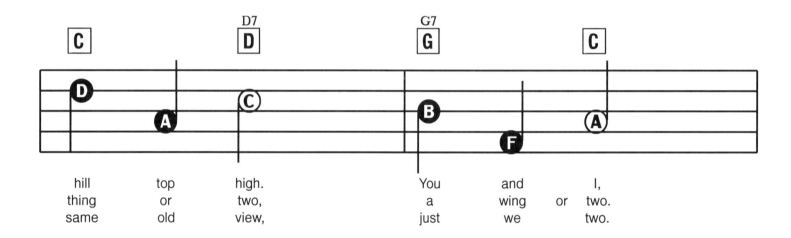

hill top high. You and I,
thing or two, a wing or two.
same old view, just we two.

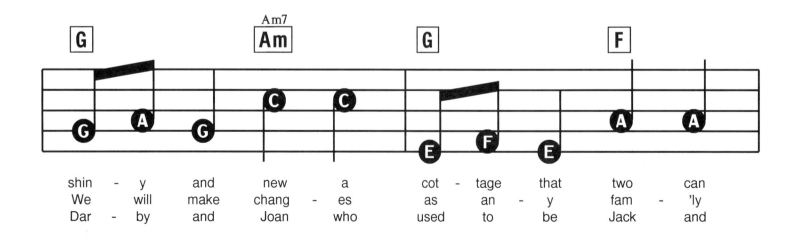

shin - y and new a cot - tage that two can
We will make chang - es as an - y two fam - 'ly
Dar - by and Joan who used to be Jack and

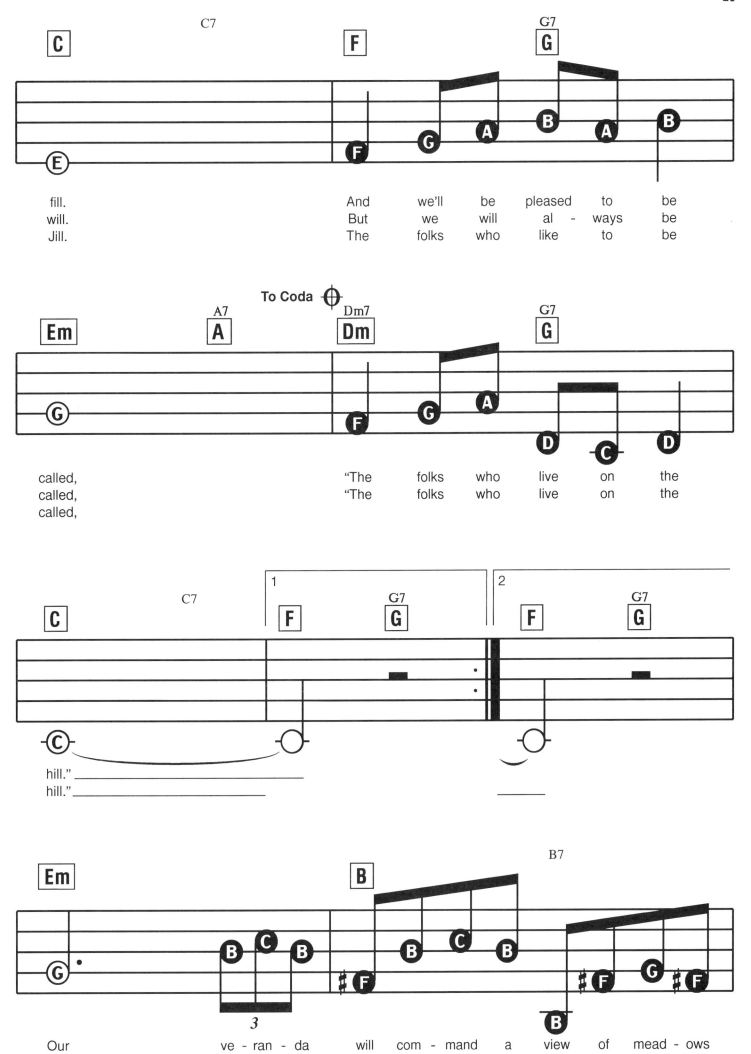

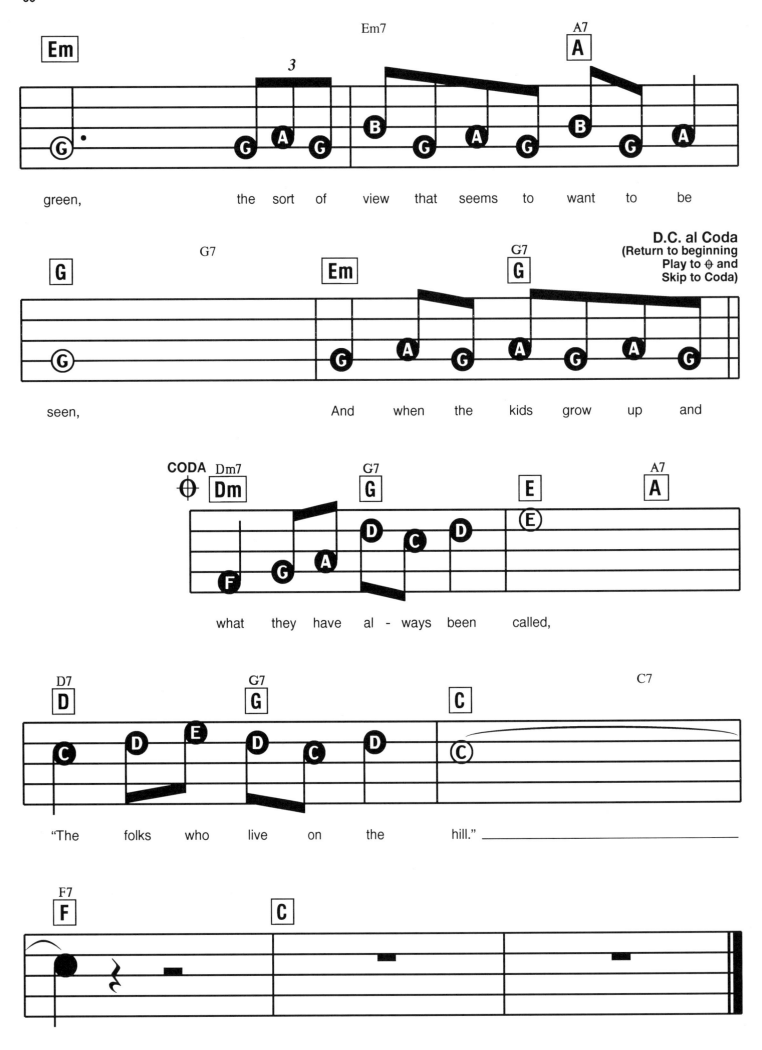

Heart and Soul
from the Paramount Short Subject A SONG IS BORN

Registration 8
Rhythm: Swing

Words by Frank Loesser
Music by Hoagy Carmichael

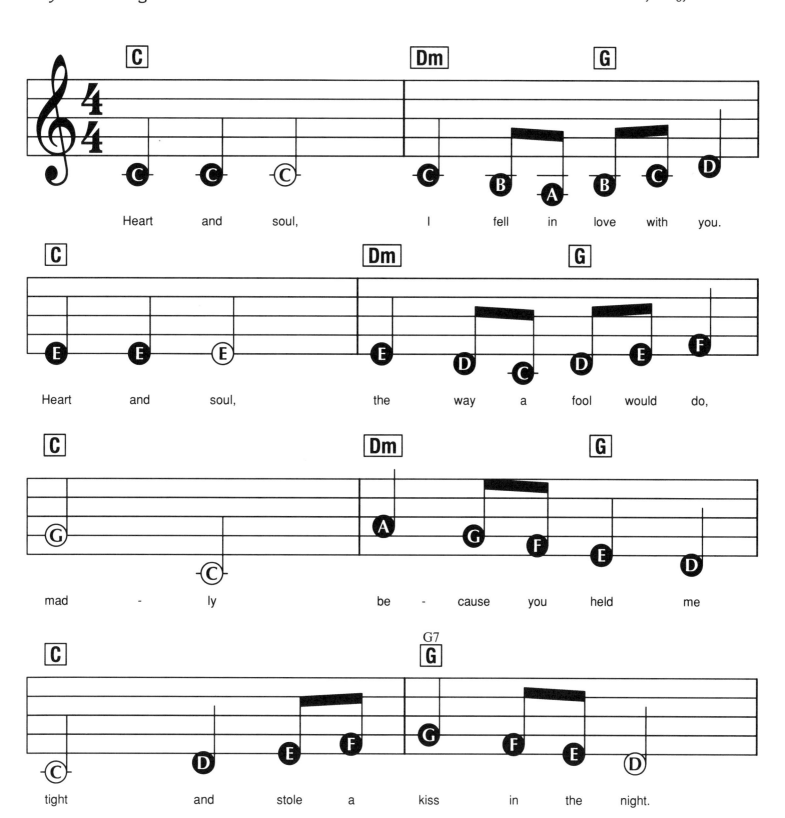

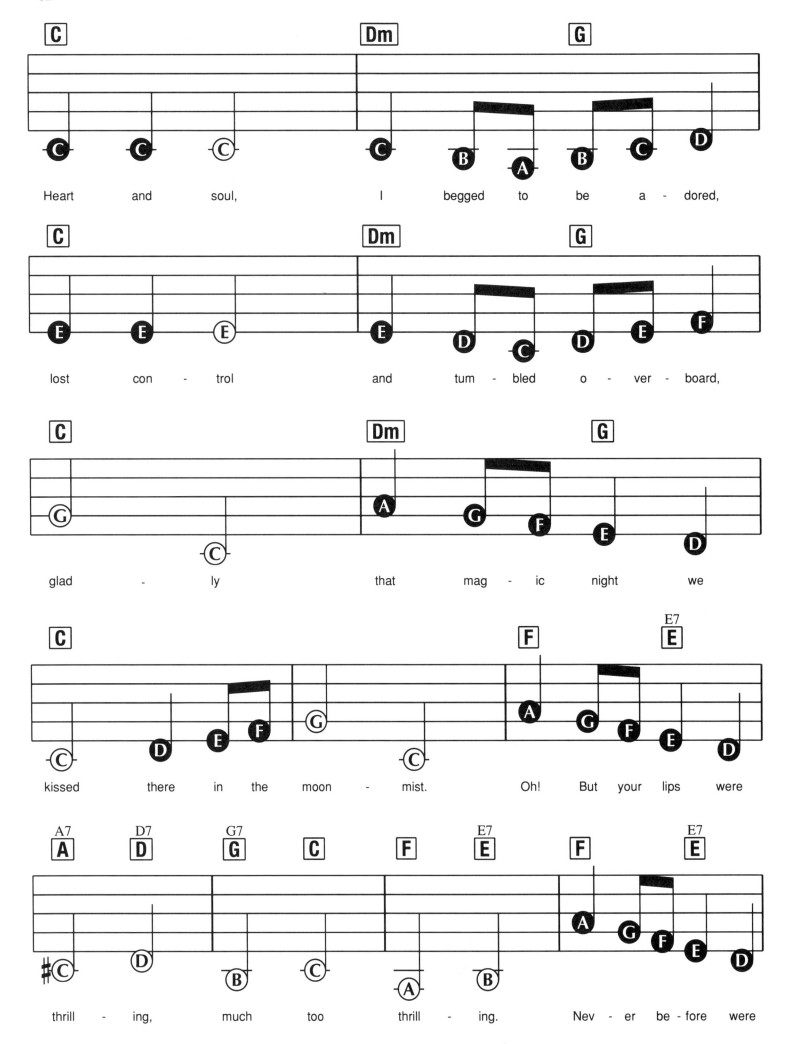

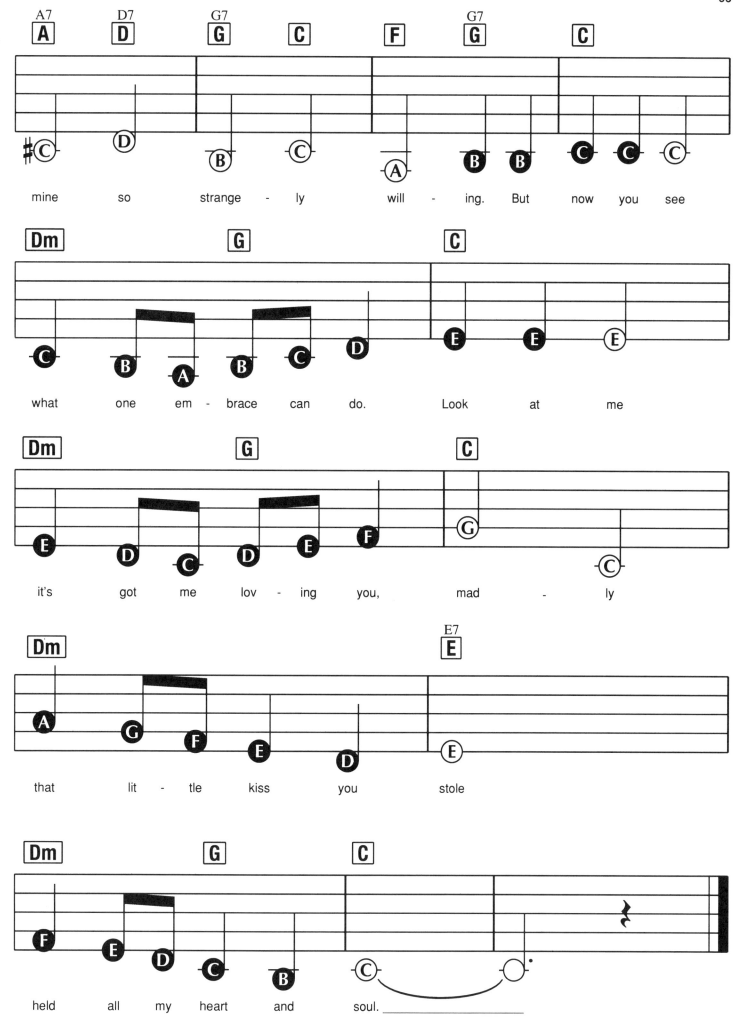

For Me and My Gal

Words by Edgar Leslie and E. Ray Goetz
Music by George W. Meyer

Registration 3
Rhythm: Swing

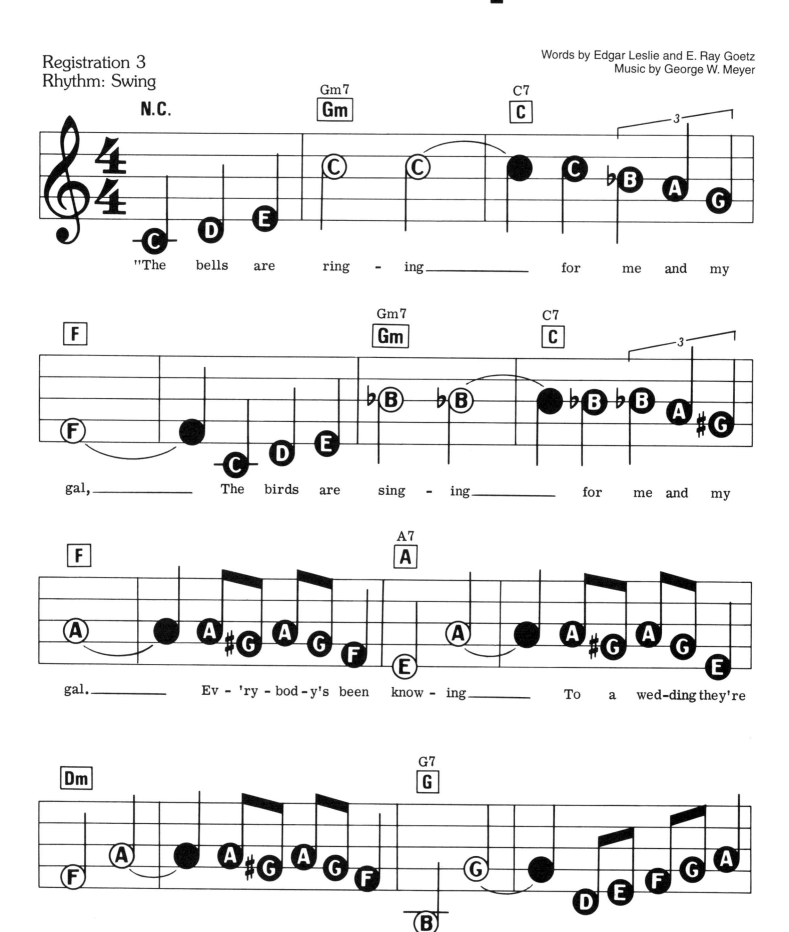

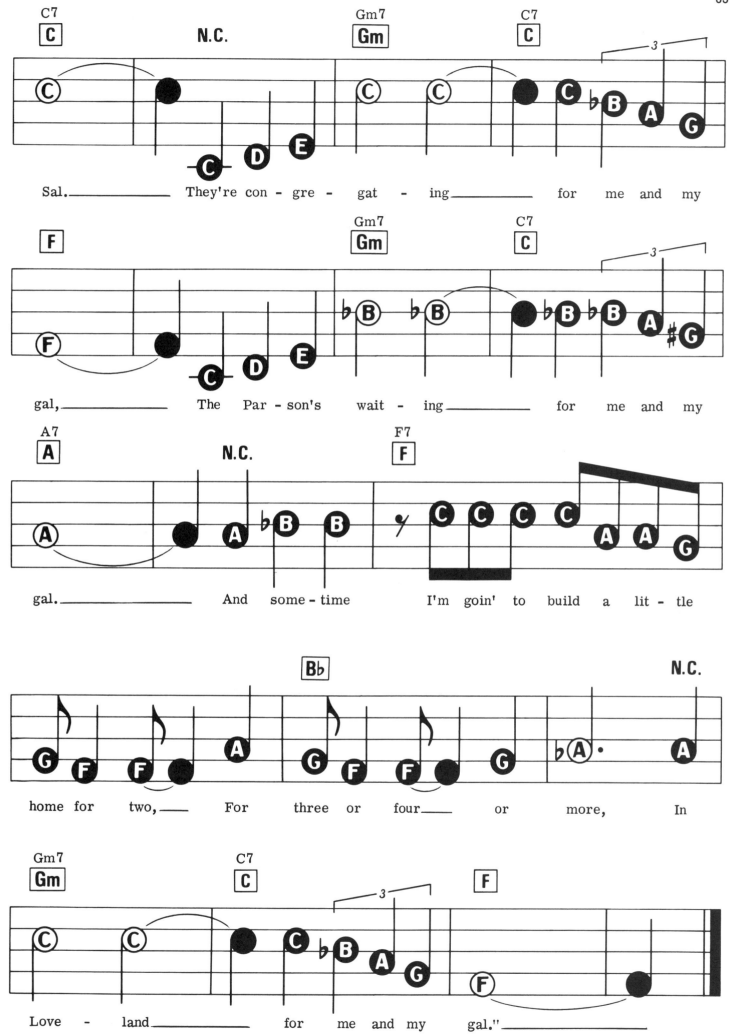

For You, For Me, For Evermore

Registration 5
Rhythm: Ballad

Music and Lyrics by George Gershwin
and Ira Gershwin

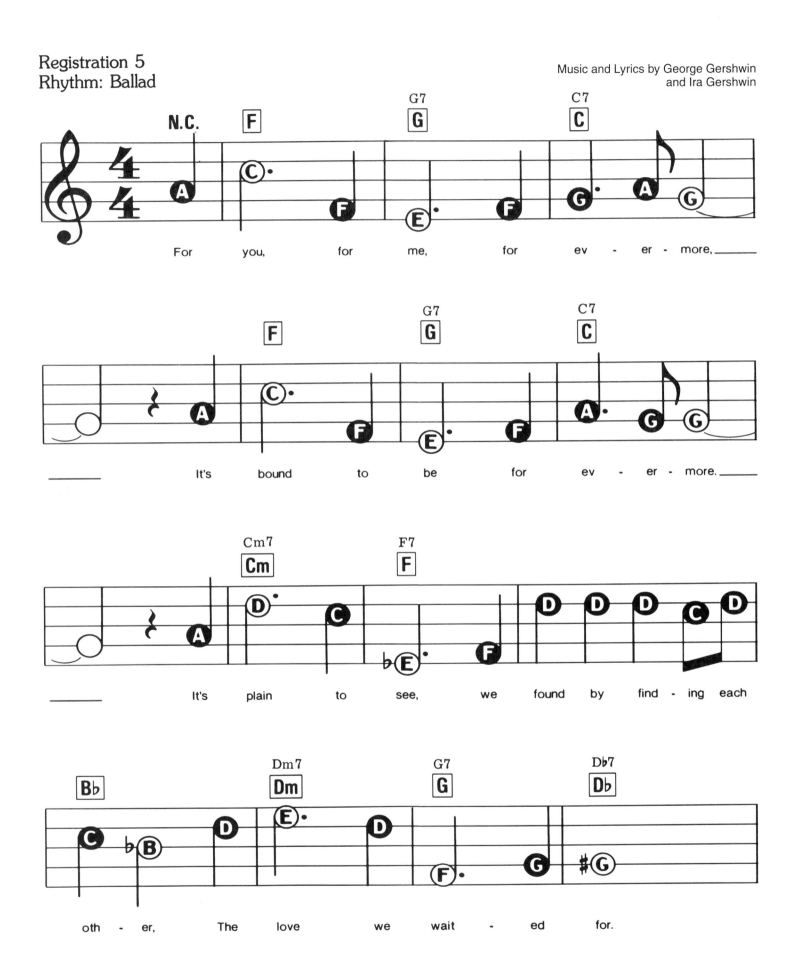

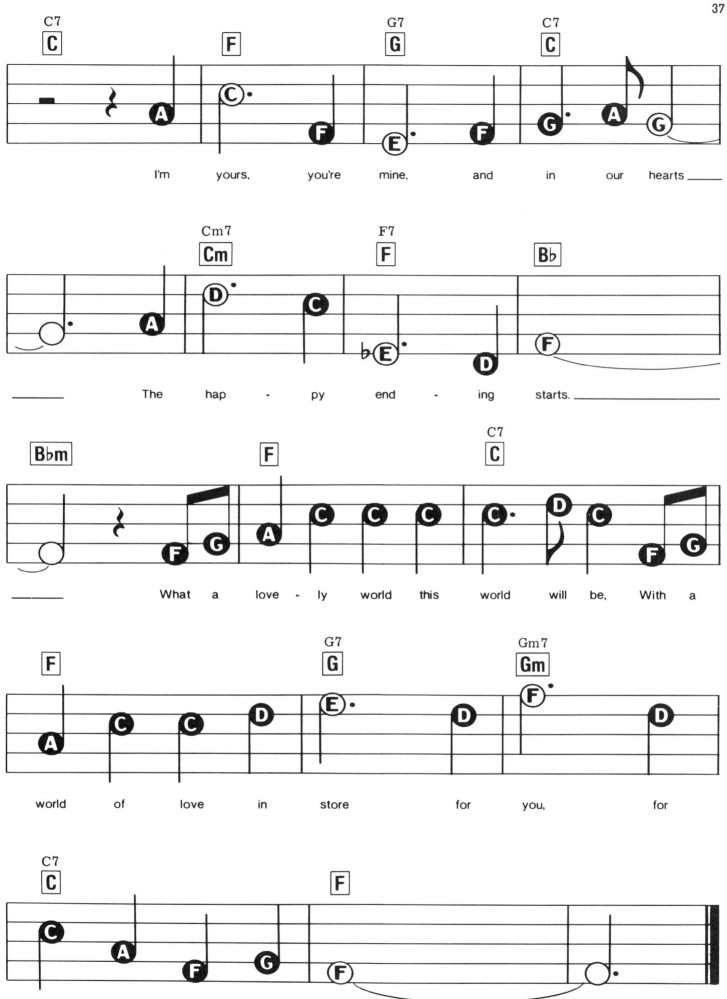

The Girl That I Marry
from the Stage Production ANNIE GET YOUR GUN

Words and Music by
Irving Berlin

Registration 2
Rhythm: Waltz

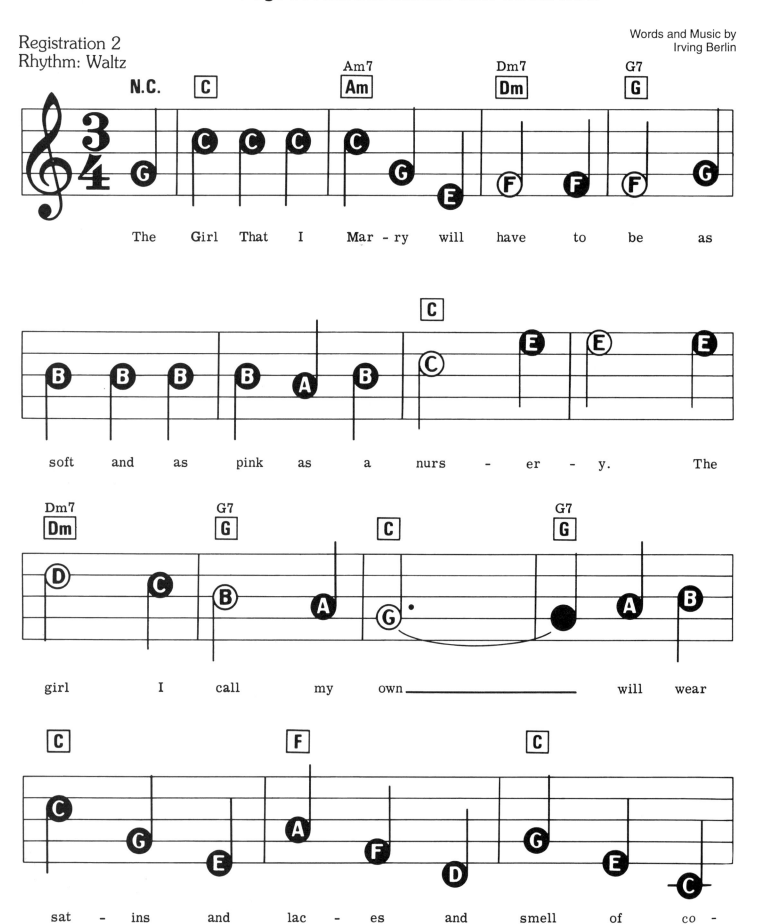

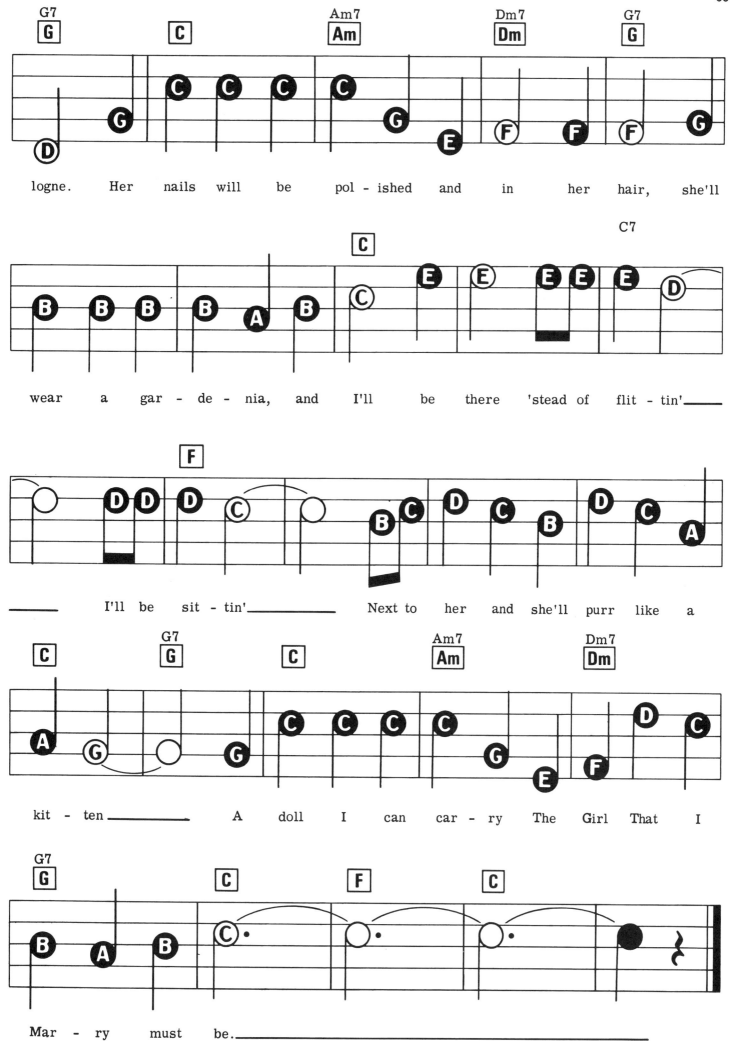

Have I Told You Lately That I Love You

Registration 10
Rhythm: Country Western or Ballad

Words and Music by
Scott Wiseman

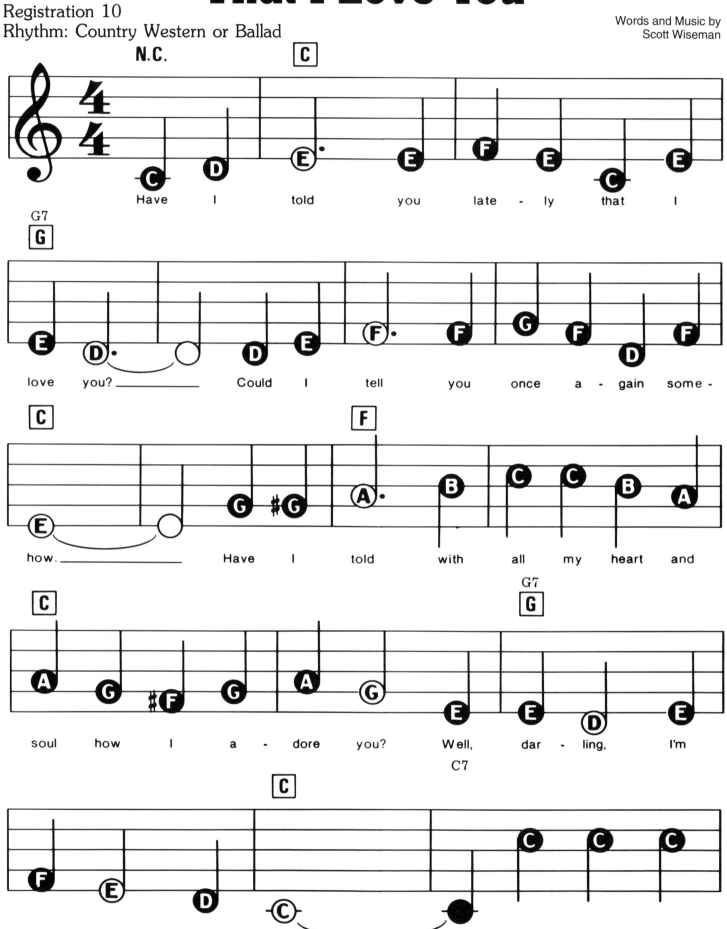

MCA Music Publishing

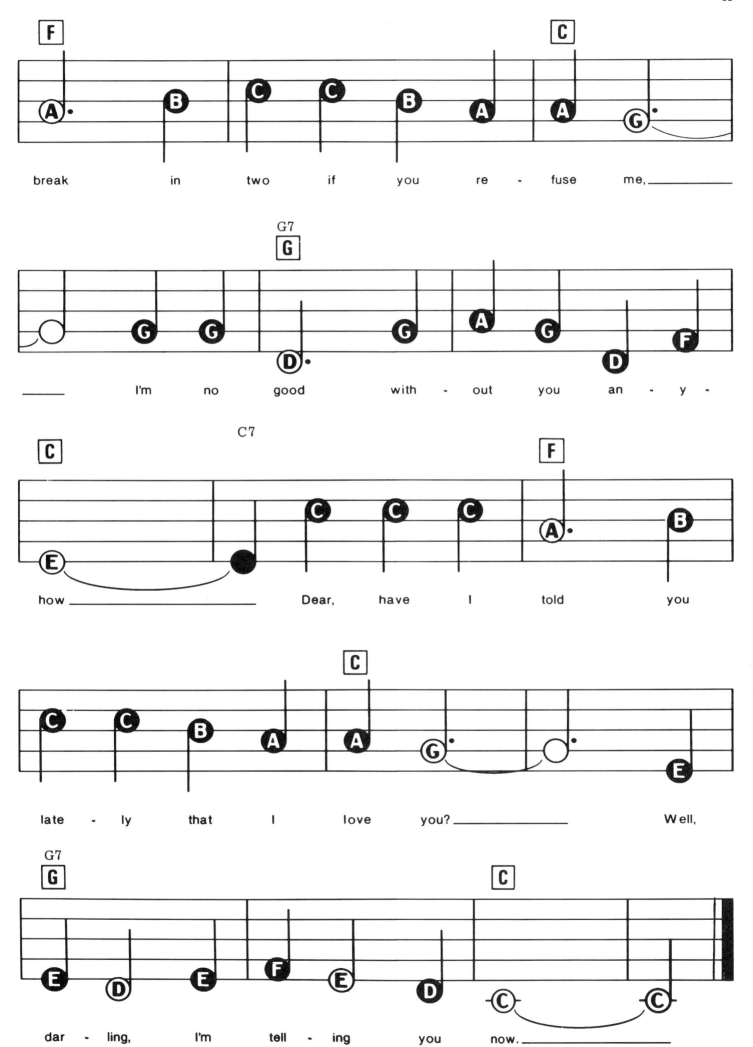

Have You Ever Been Lonely?
(Have You Ever Been Blue?)

Registration 3
Rhythm: Swing or Jazz

Words by George Brown
Music by Peter DeRose

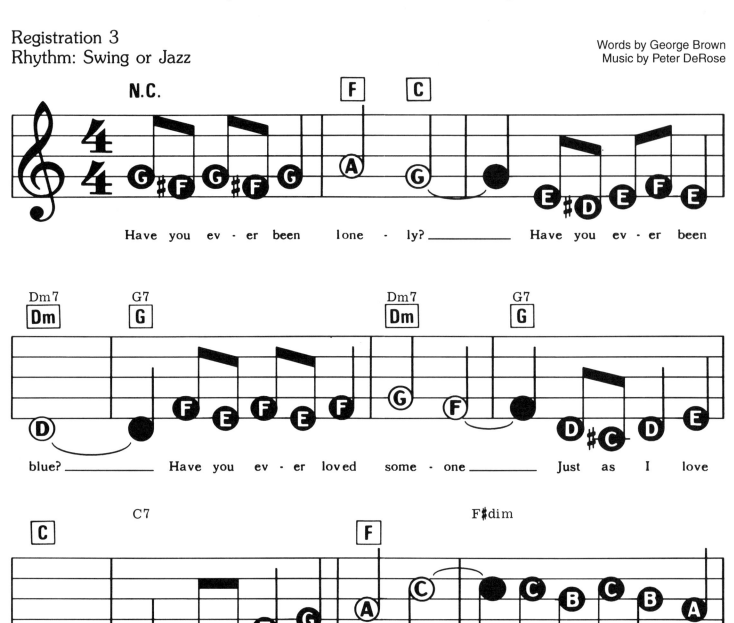

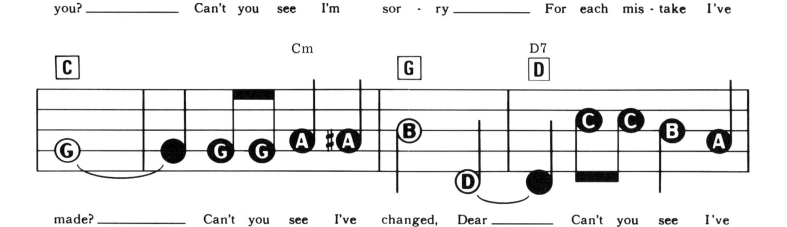

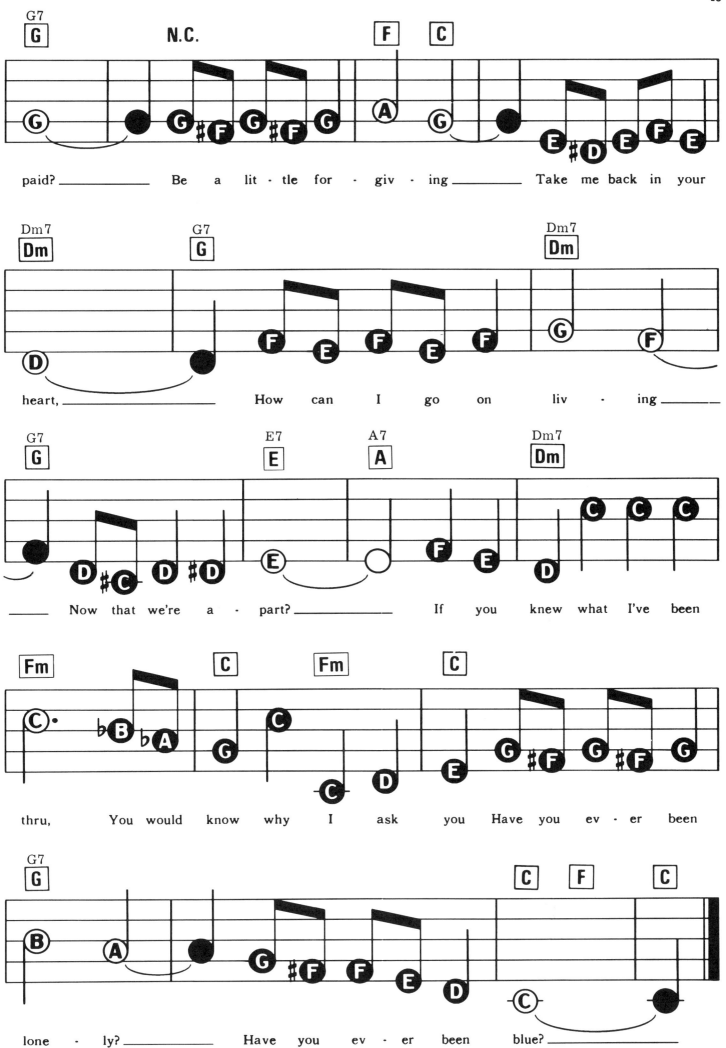

The Hawaiian Wedding Song
(Ke Kali Nei Au)

Registration 10
Rhythm: Fox Trot or Swing

English Lyrics by Al Hoffman and Dick Manning
Hawaiian Lyrics and Music by Charles E. King

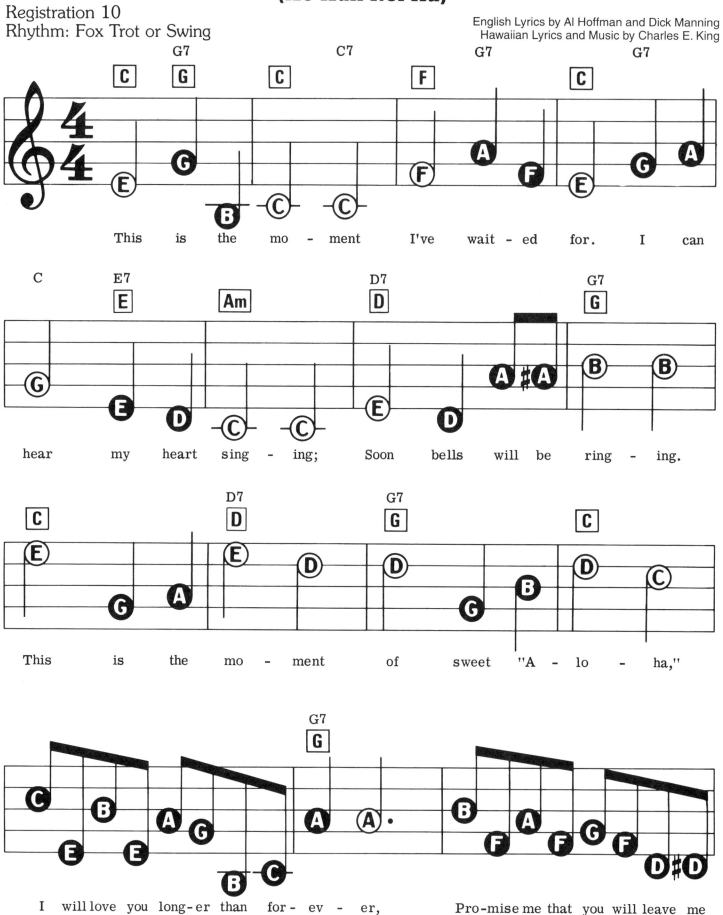

MCA Music Publishing

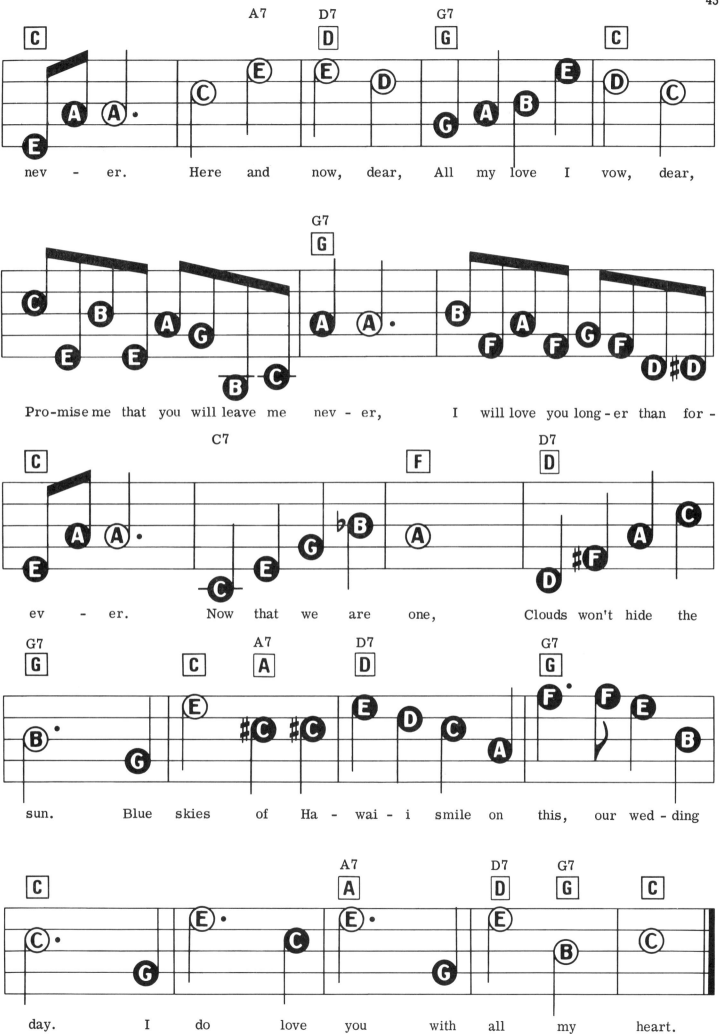

Honey
(I'm in Love with You)

Registration 8
Rhythm: Fox Trot or Swing

Words and Music by Seymour Simons,
Haven Gillespie and Richard A. Whiting

The Last Waltz

Words and Music by Les Reed
and Barry Mason

Registration 4
Rhythm: Waltz

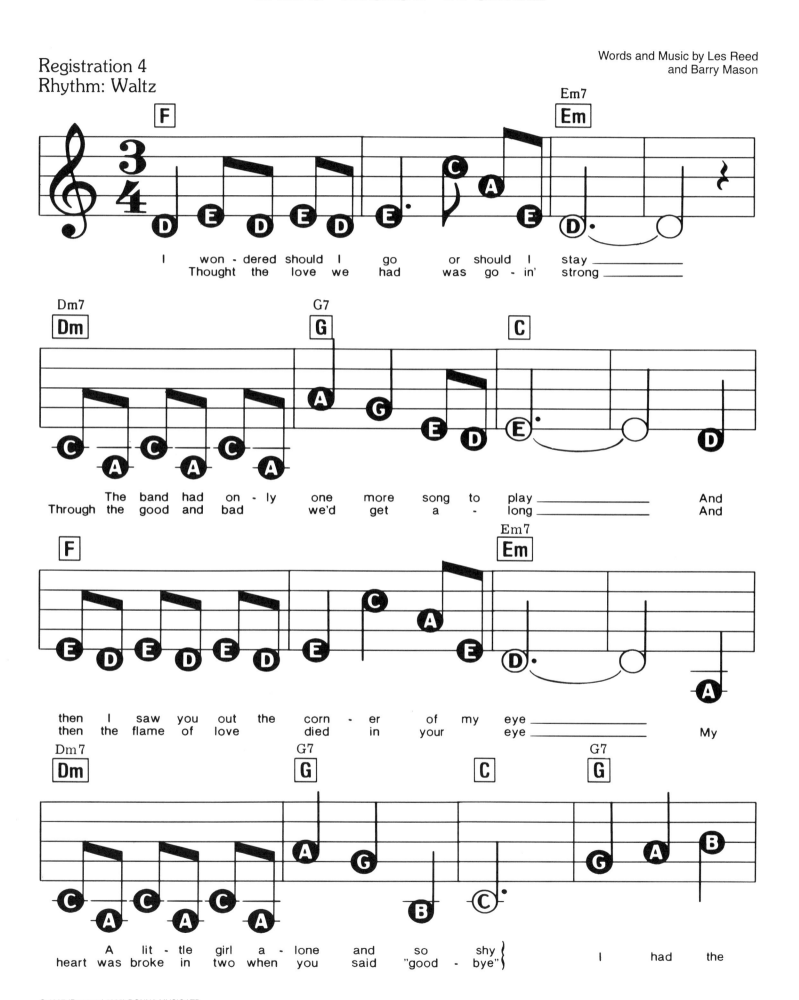

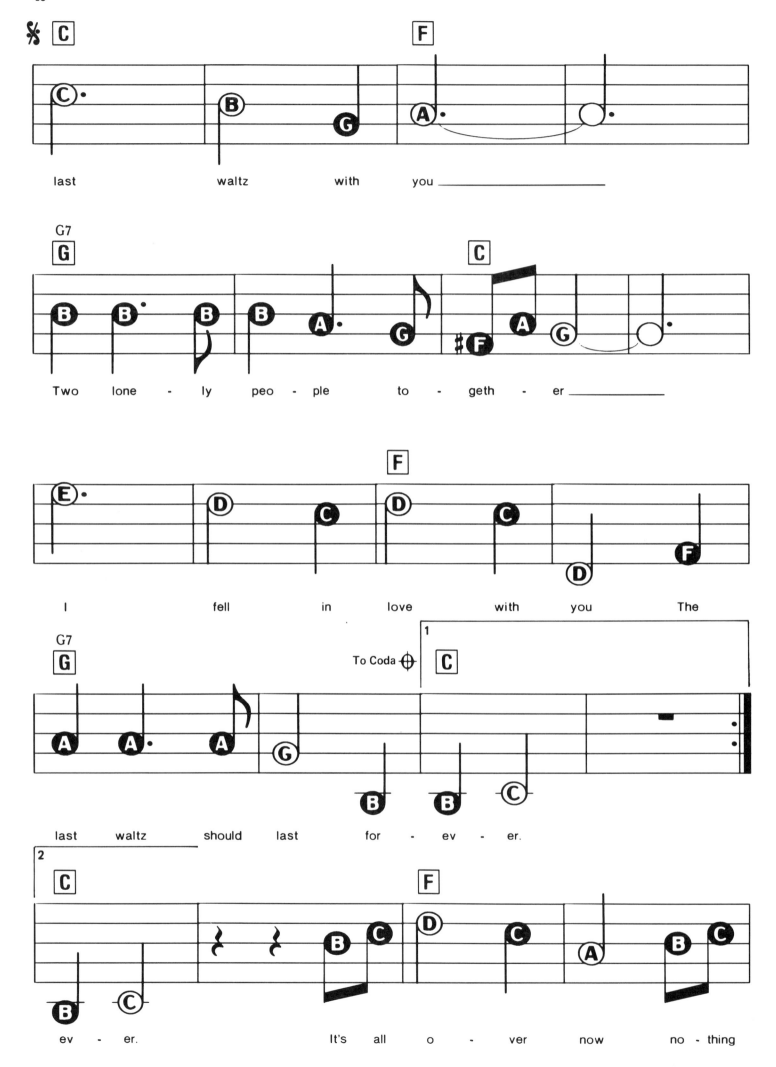

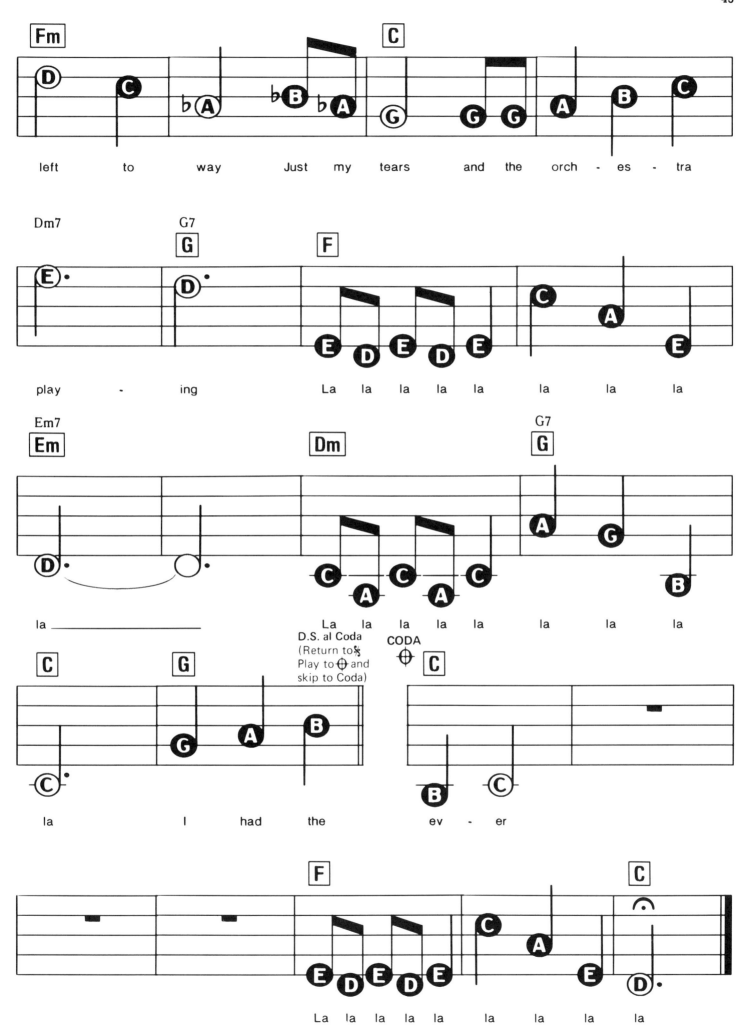

How Deep Is the Ocean
(How High Is the Sky)

Registration 4
Rhythm: Fox Trot or Swing

Words and Music by
Irving Berlin

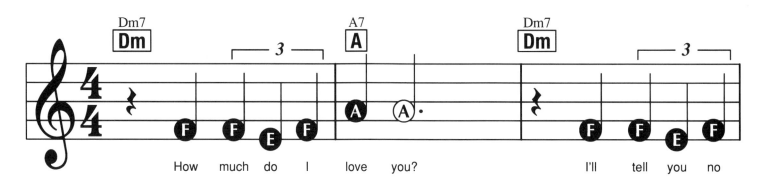

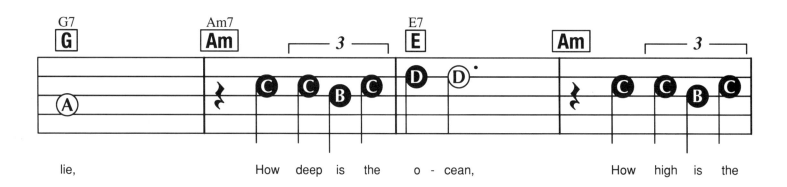

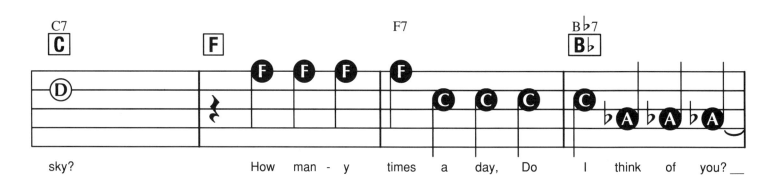

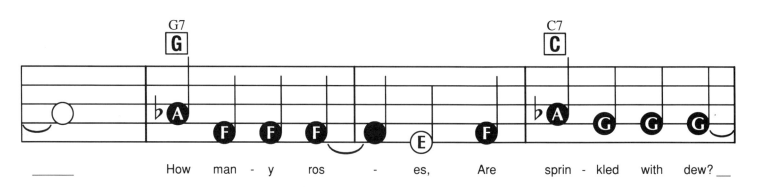

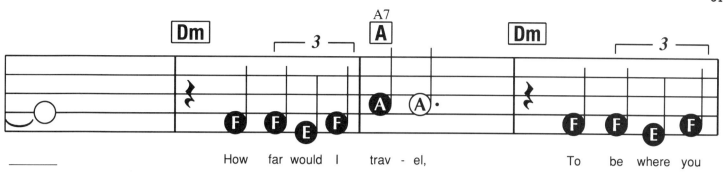

How far would I trav-el, To be where you

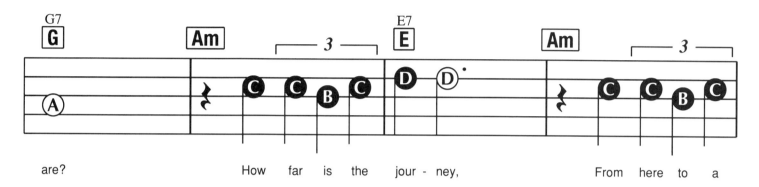

are? How far is the jour-ney, From here to a

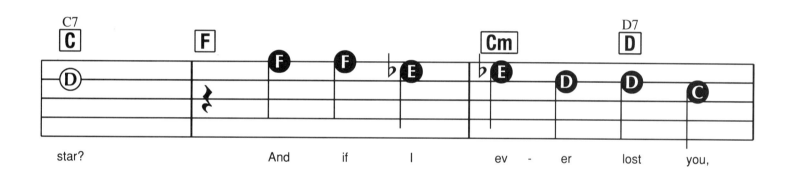

star? And if I ev-er lost you,

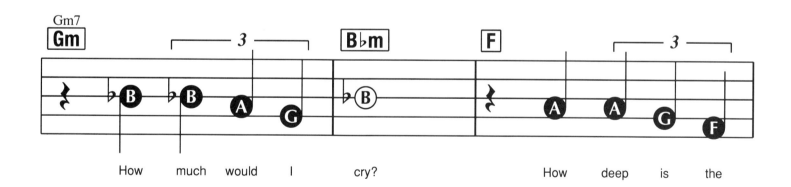

How much would I cry? How deep is the

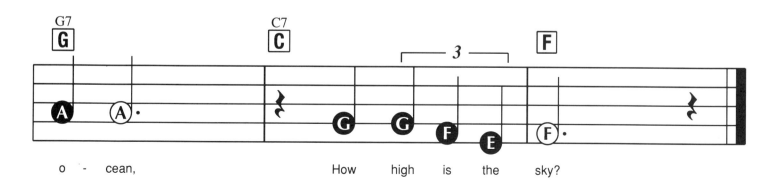

o-cean, How high is the sky?

I Can't Give You Anything But Love

from BLACKBIRDS OF 1928

Registration 5
Rhythm: Swing or Jazz

Words by Dorothy Fields
Music by Jimmy McHugh

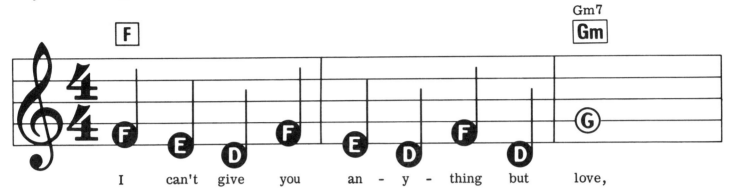

I can't give you an - y - thing but love,

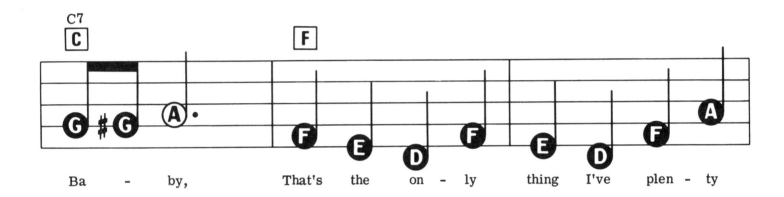

Ba - by, That's the on - ly thing I've plen - ty

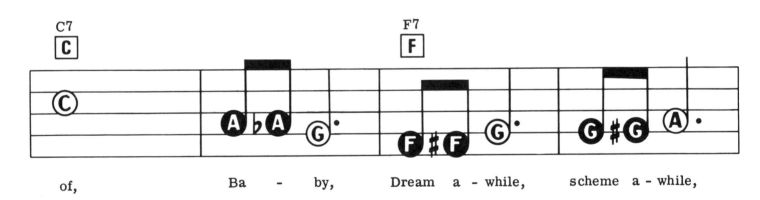

of, Ba - by, Dream a - while, scheme a - while,

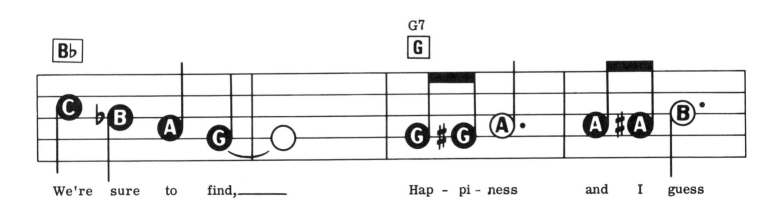

We're sure to find,_____ Hap - pi - ness and I guess

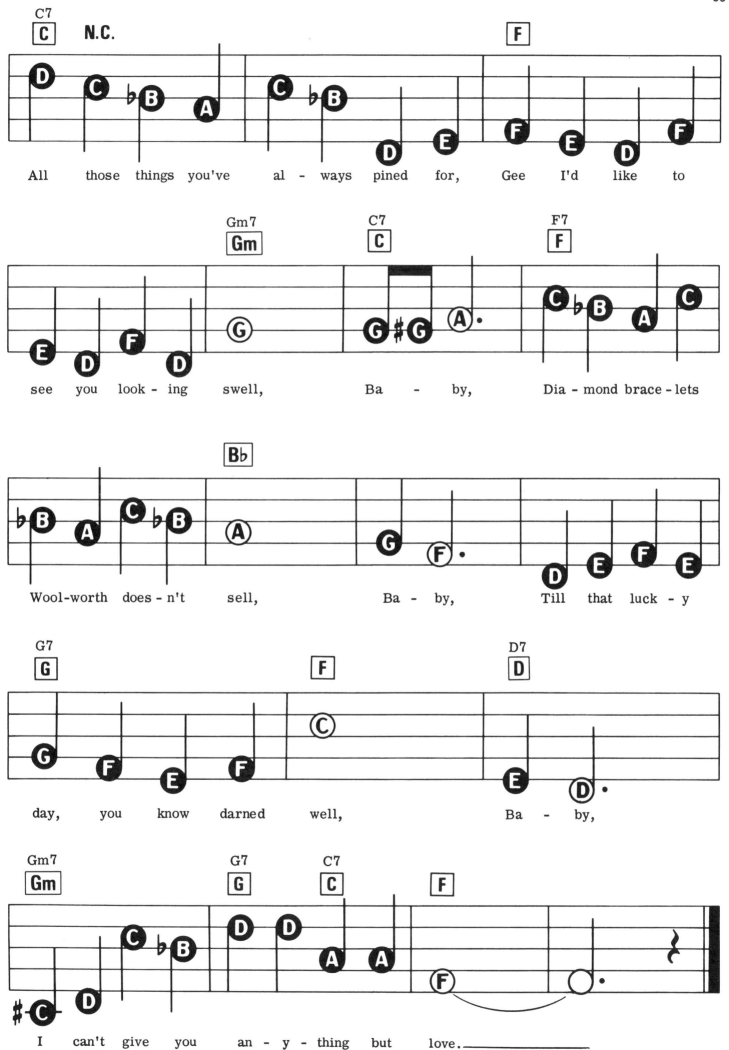

I Don't Know Why

(I Just Do)

Registration 8
Rhythm: Fox Trot or Swing

Lyric by Roy Turk
Music by Fred E. Ahlert

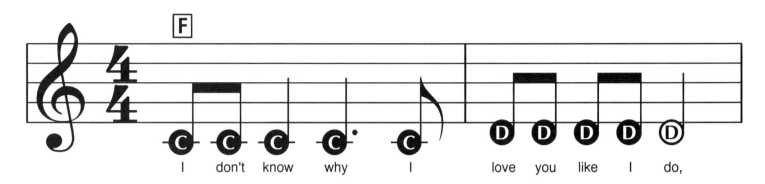

I don't know why I love you like I do,

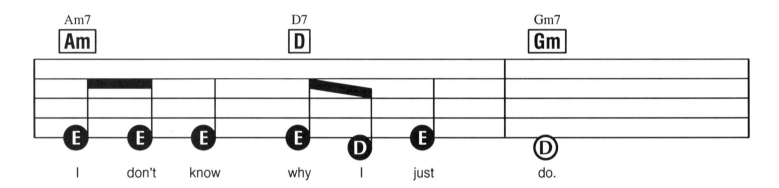

I don't know why I just do.

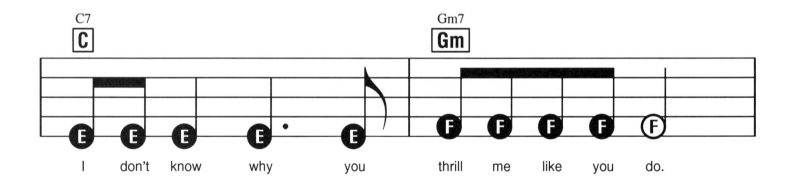

I don't know why you thrill me like you do.

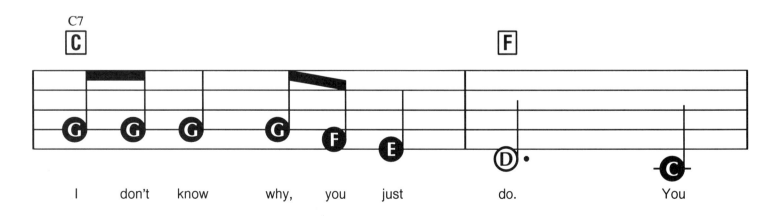

I don't know why, you just do. You

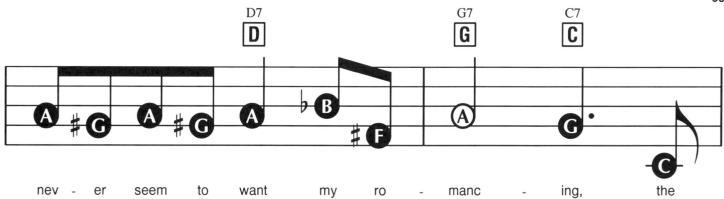

nev - er seem to want my ro - manc - ing, the

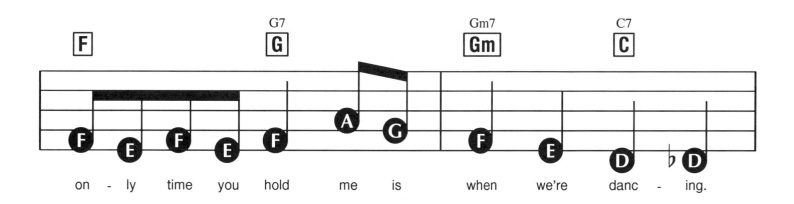

on - ly time you hold me is when we're danc - ing.

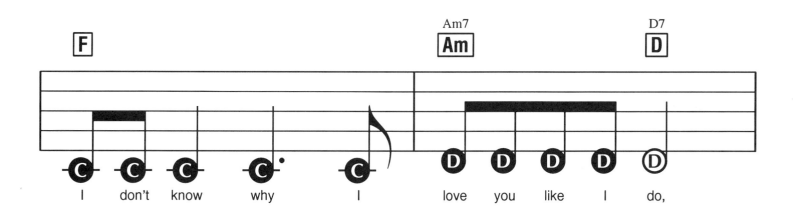

I don't know why I love you like I do,

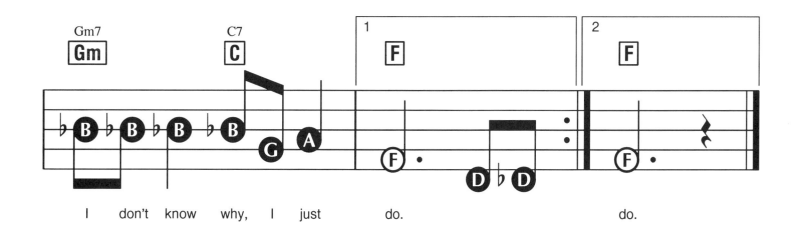

I don't know why, I just do. do.

I Love You Truly

Registration 10
Rhythm: Waltz

Words and Music by
Carrie Jacobs-Bond

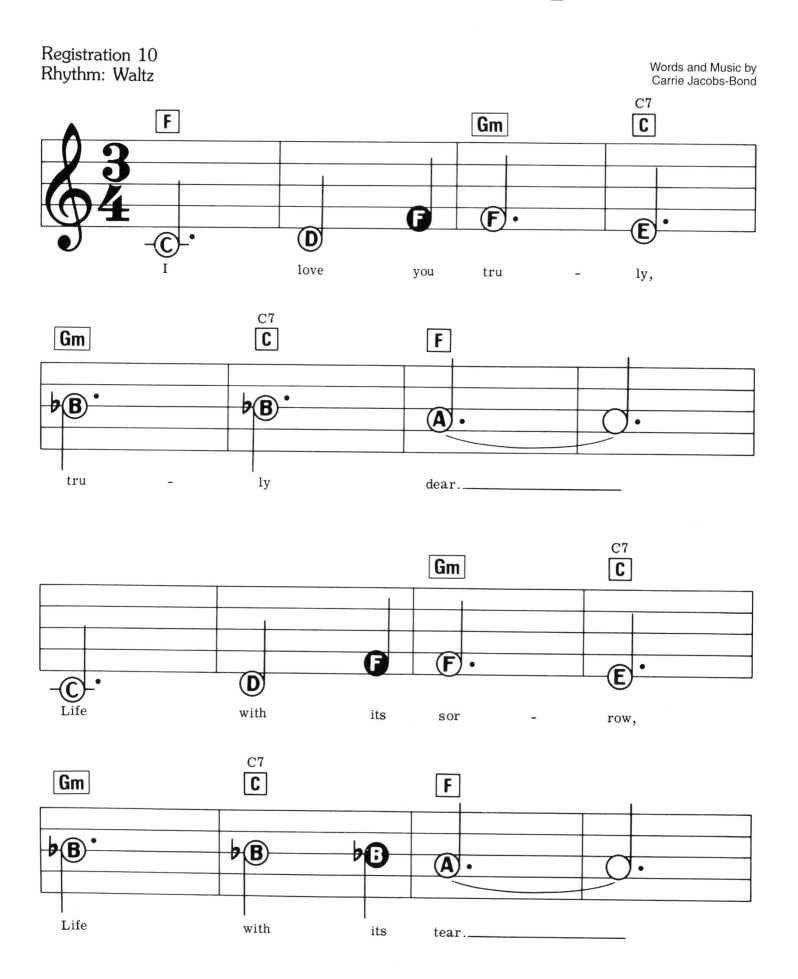

57

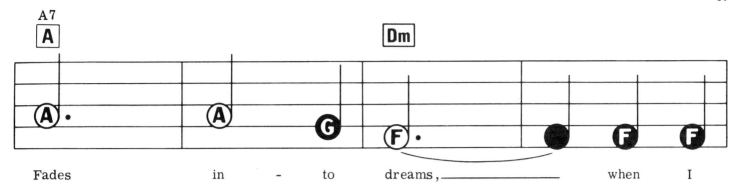

Fades   in - to   to   dreams,_____   when   I

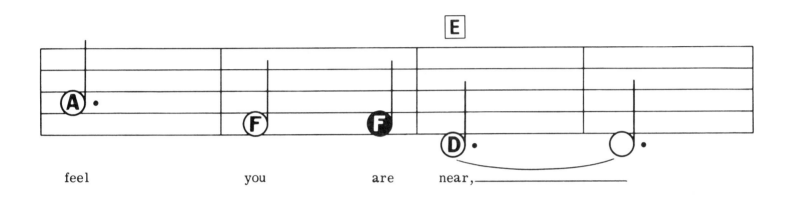

feel   you   are   near,_____

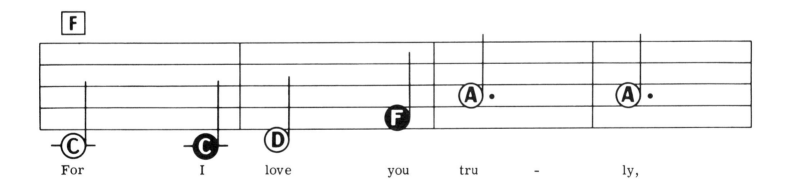

For   I   love   you   tru   -   ly,

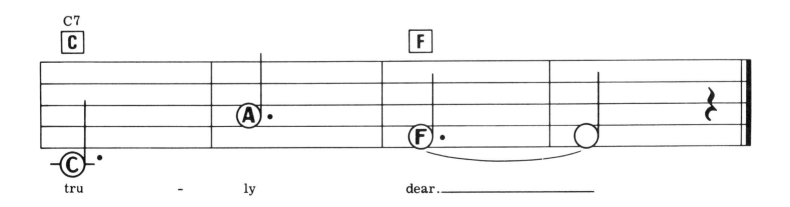

tru   -   ly   dear._____

I'm Old Fashioned
from YOU WERE NEVER LOVELIER

Registration 5
Rhythm: Fox Trot or Swing

Words by Johnny Mercer
Music by Jerome Kern

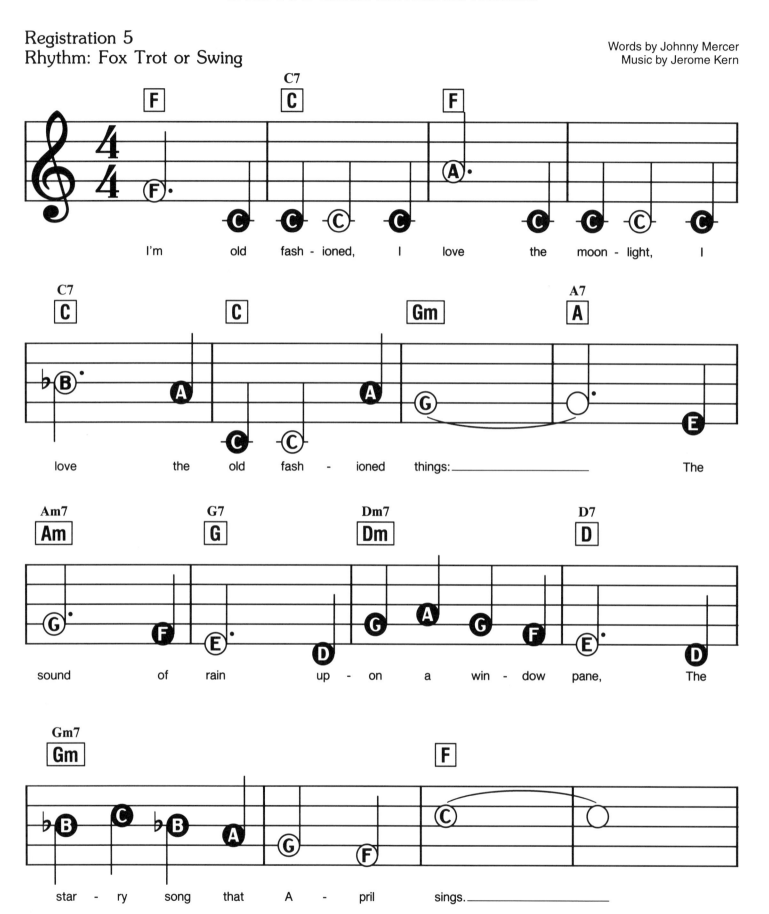

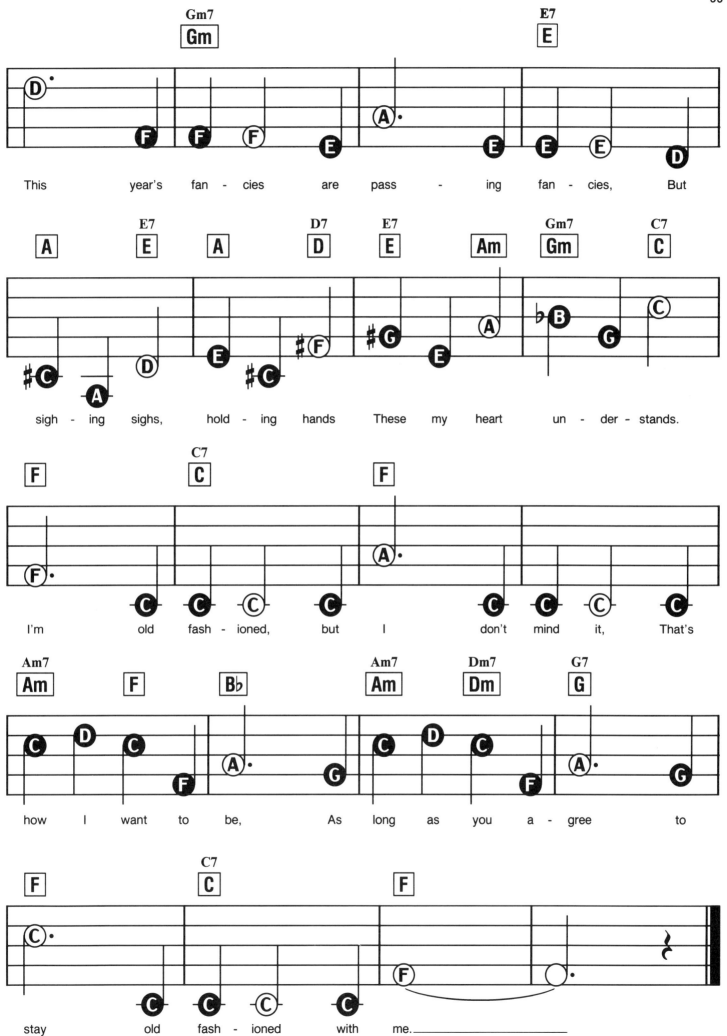

If You Were the Only Girl
in the World

Registration 10
Rhythm: Waltz

Words by Clifford Grey
Music by Nat D. Ayer

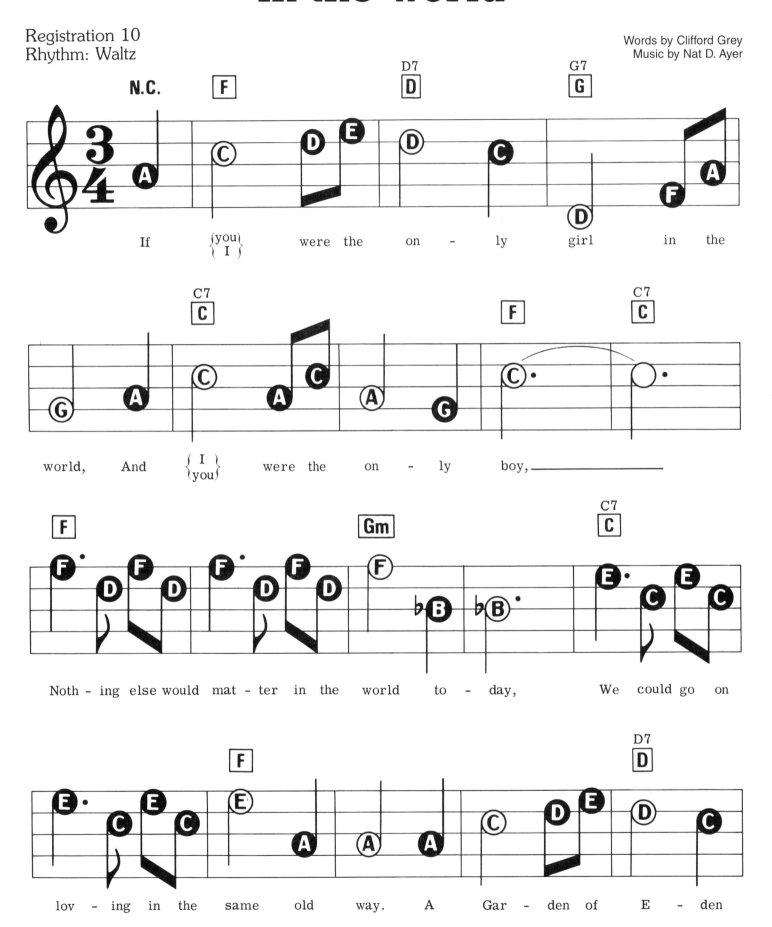

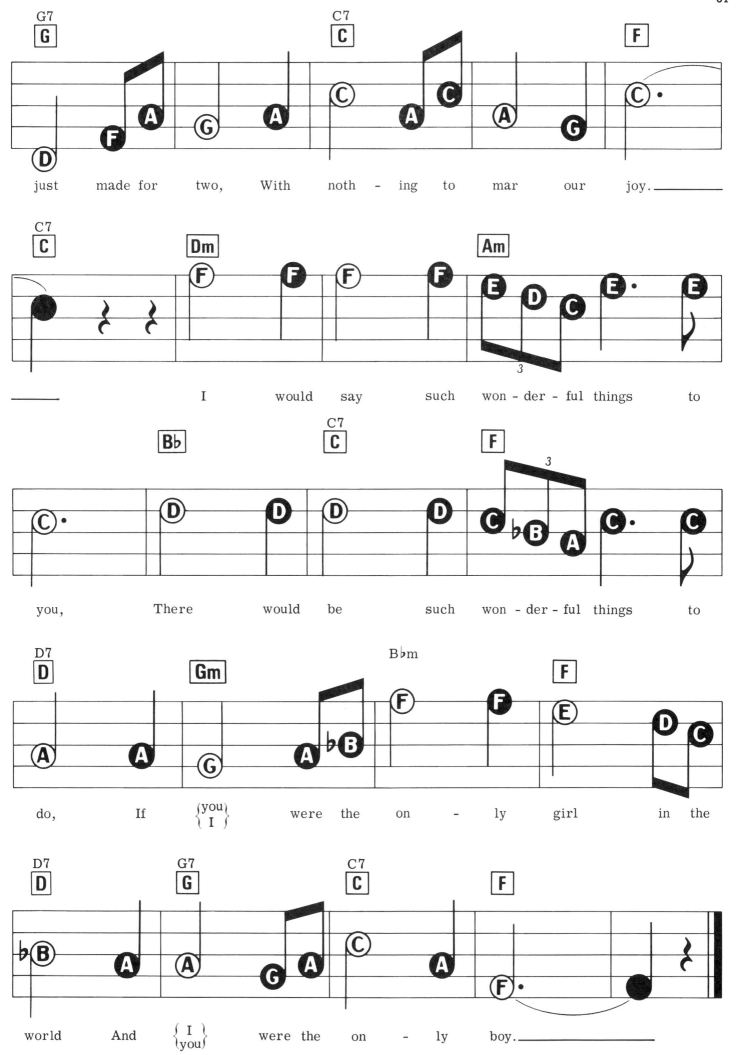

61

Let Me Call You Sweetheart

Words by Beth Slater Whitson
Music by Leo Friedman

Registration 3
Rhythm: Waltz

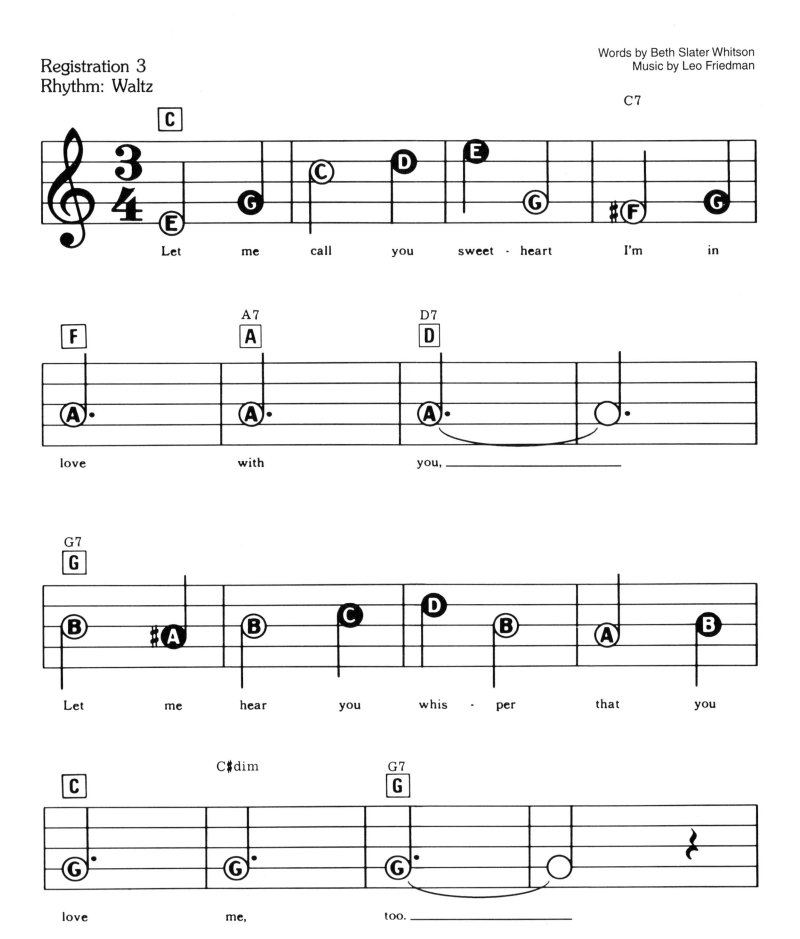

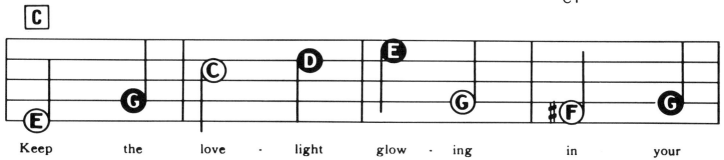

Keep the love - light glow - ing in your

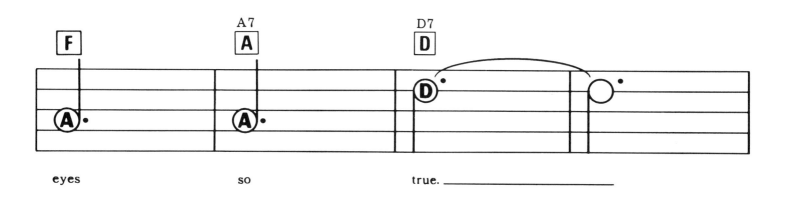

eyes so true. _____

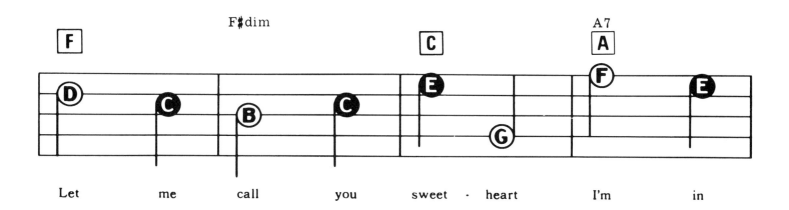

Let me call you sweet - heart I'm in

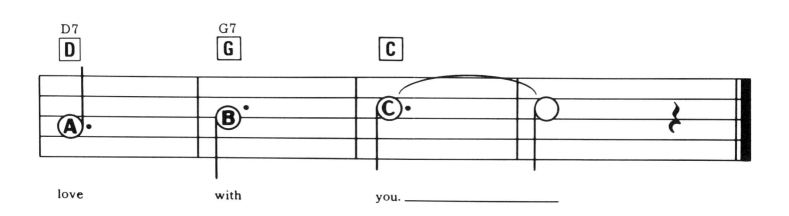

love with you. _____

Love Letters
Theme from the Paramount Picture LOVE LETTERS

Registration 1
Rhythm: Swing

Words by Edward Heyman
Music by Victor Young

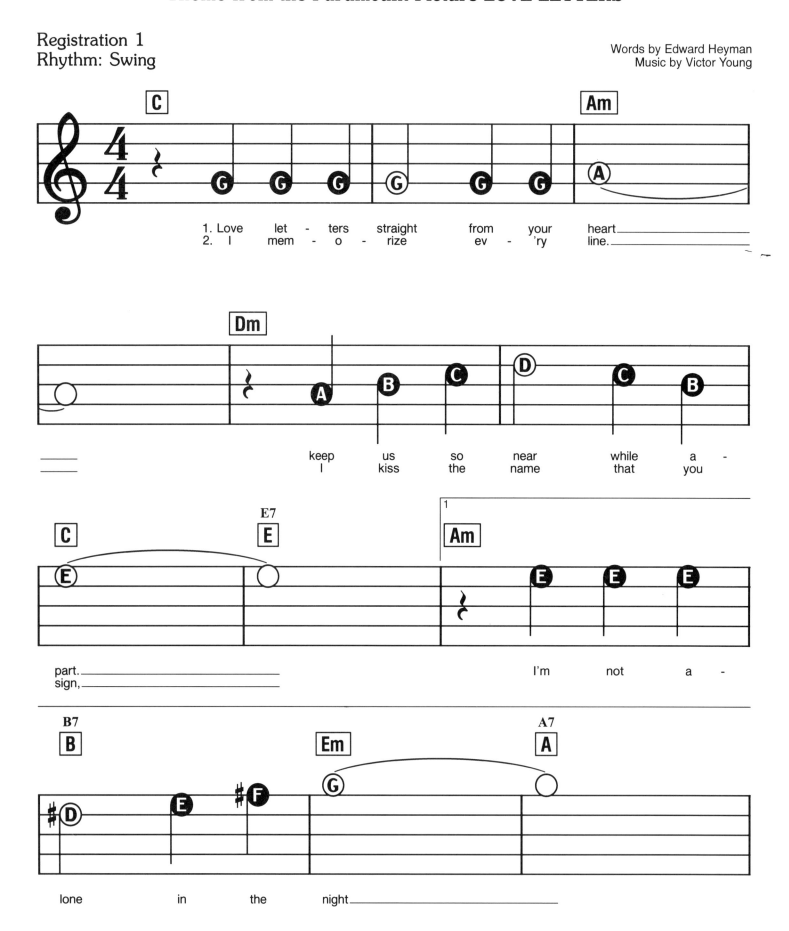

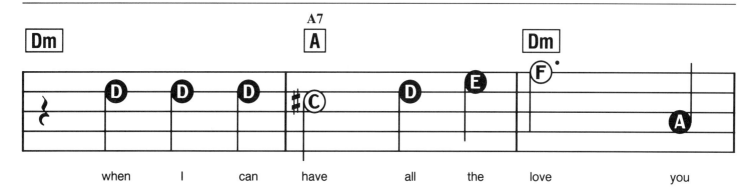

when I can have all the love you

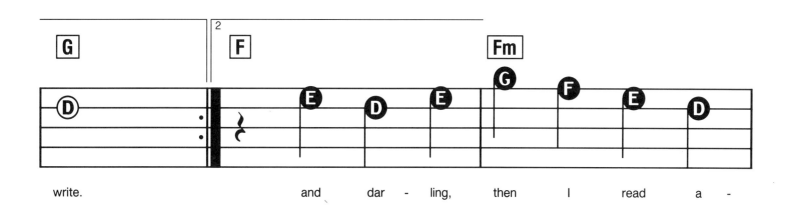

write. and dar - ling, then I read a -

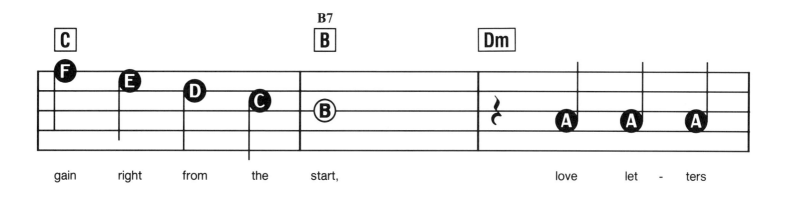

gain right from the start, love let - ters

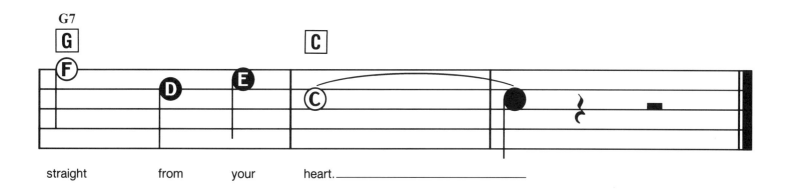

straight from your heart.

Melody of Love

Registration 10
Rhythm: Waltz

Lyric by Tom Glazer
Music by H. Engelmann

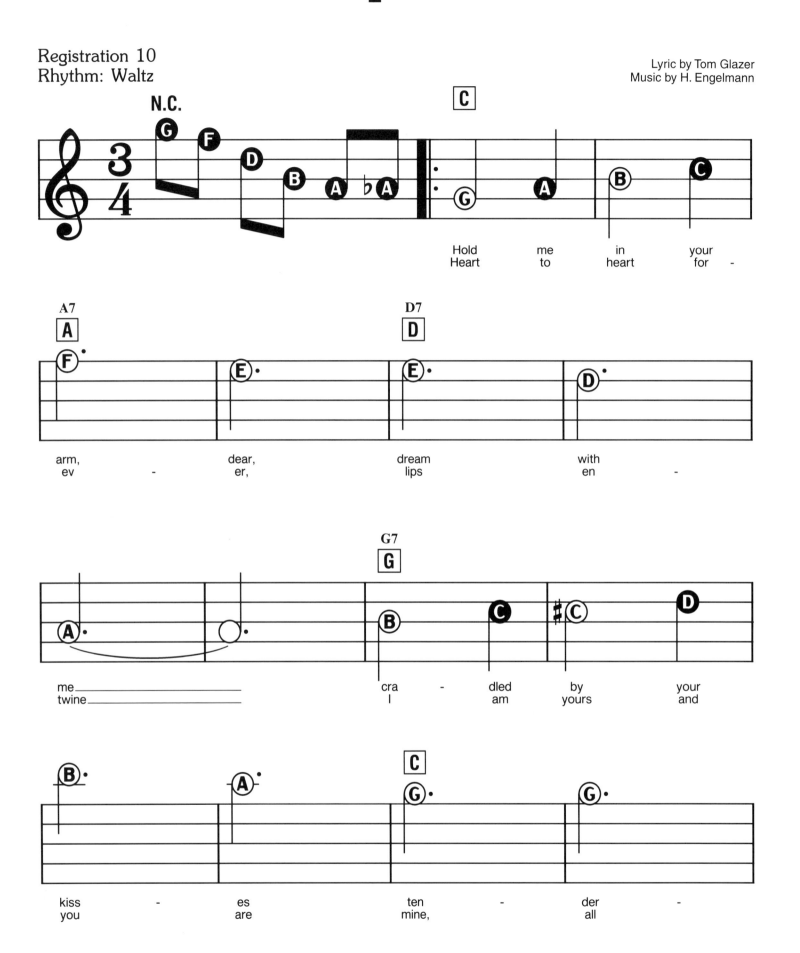

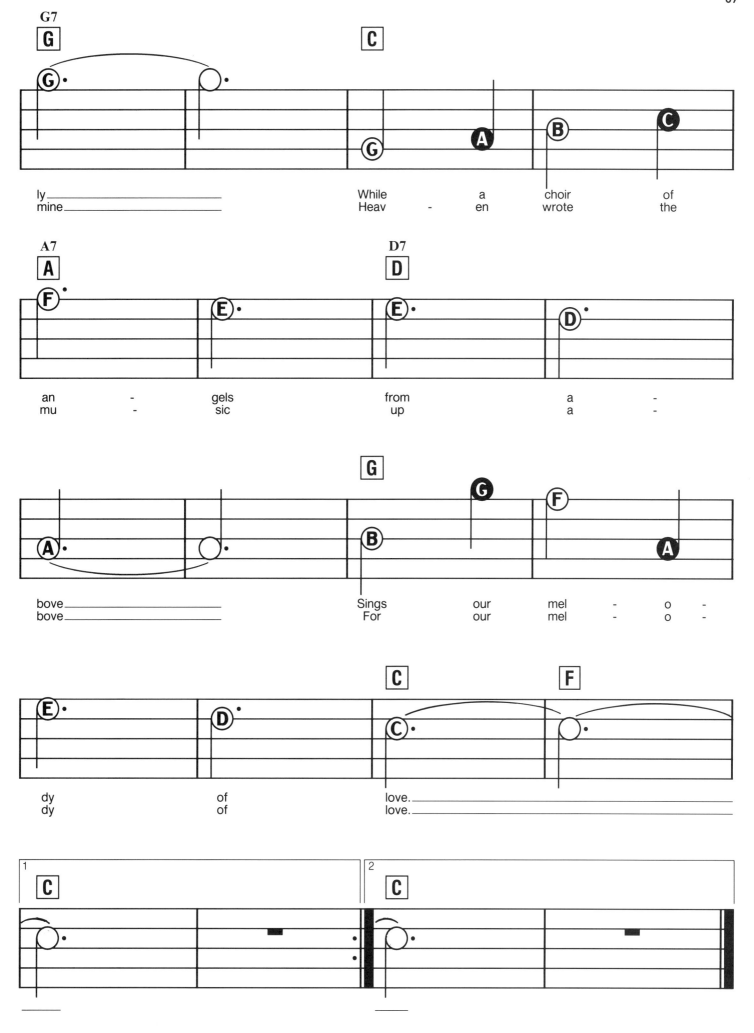

Moonlight and Roses
(Bring Mem'ries of You)

Registration 9
Rhythm: Ballad or Fox Trot

Words and Music by Ben Black,
Edwin H. Lemare and Neil Moret

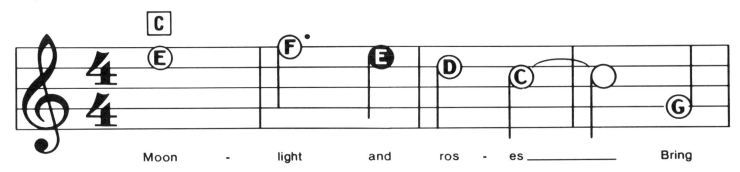

Moon - light and ros - es _____ Bring

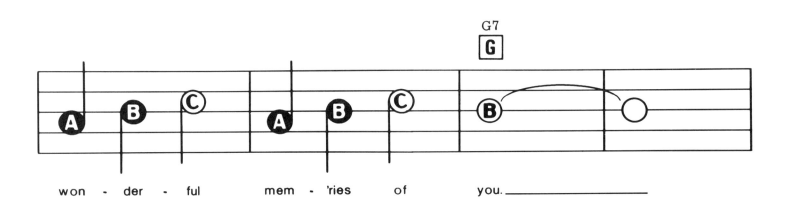

won - der - ful mem - 'ries of you. _____

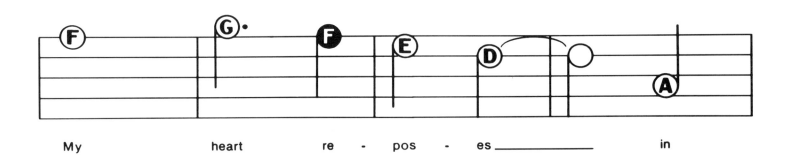

My heart re - pos - es _____ in

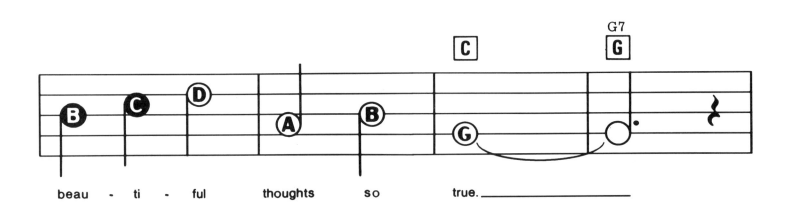

beau - ti - ful thoughts so true. _____

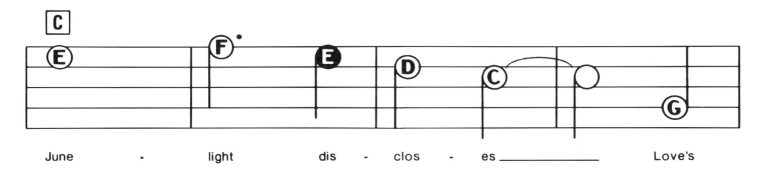

June - light dis - clos - es _____ Love's

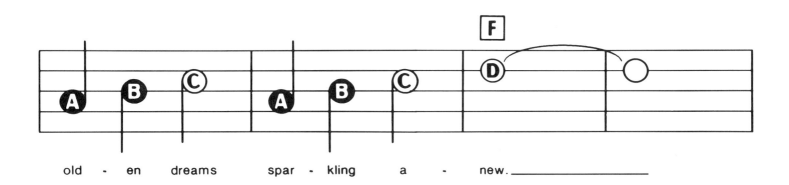

old - en dreams spar - kling a - new. _____

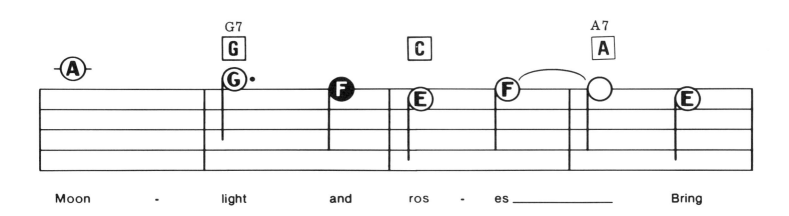

Moon - light and ros - es _____ Bring

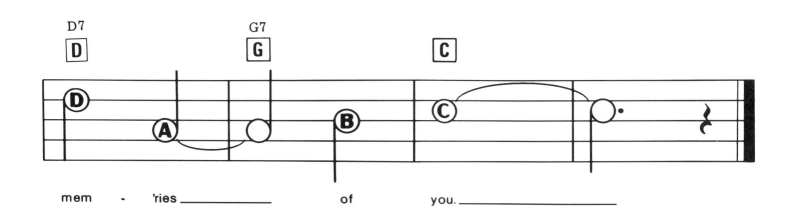

mem - 'ries _____ of you. _____

My Baby Just Cares for Me

Registration 4
Rhythm: Swing or Jazz

Lyrics by Gus Kahn
Music by Walter Donaldson

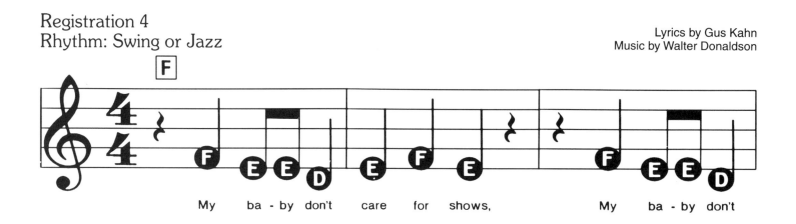

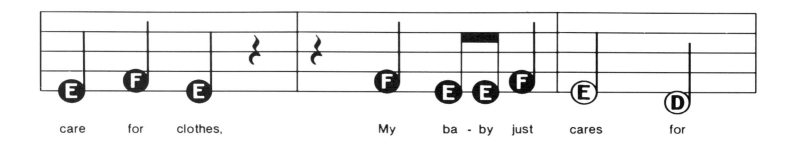

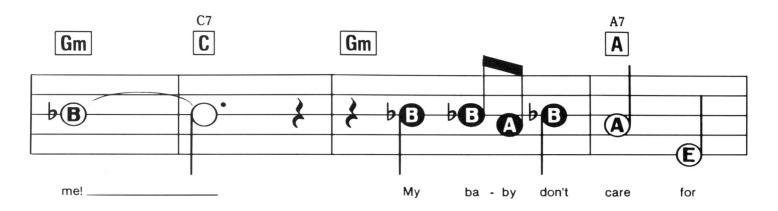

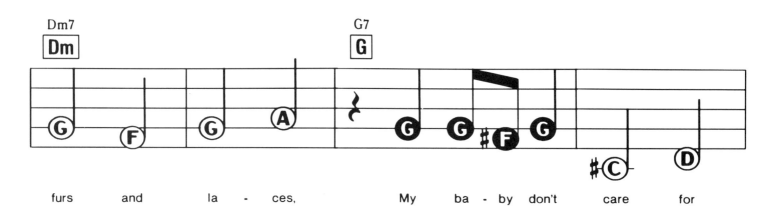

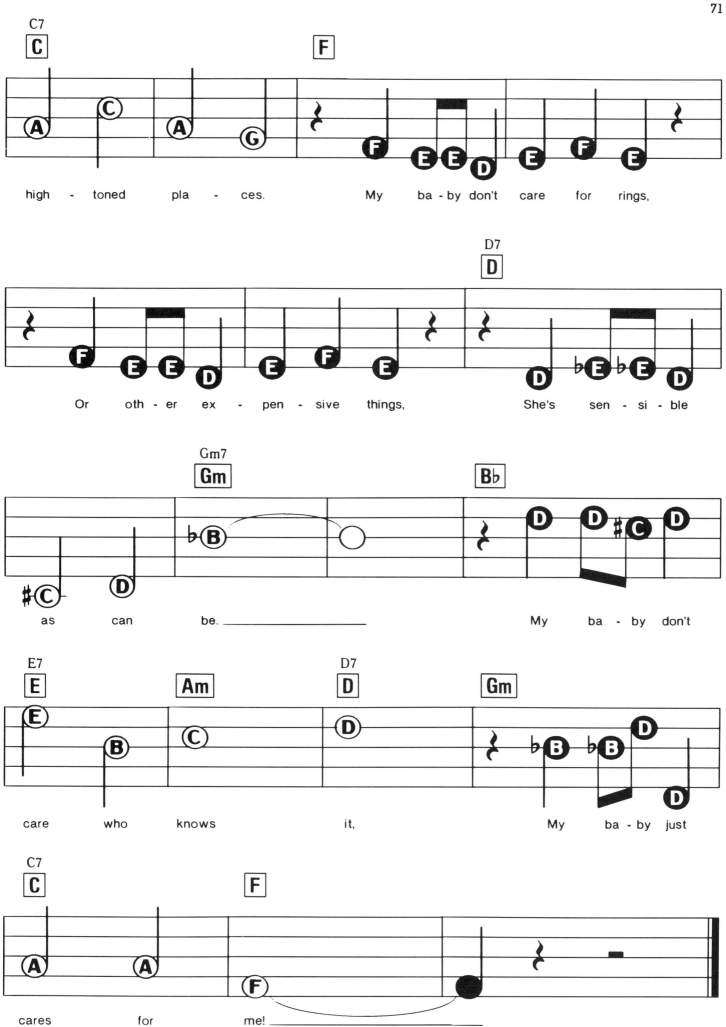

My Blue Heaven

Registration 9
Rhythm: Swing

Lyric by George Whiting
Music by Walter Donaldson

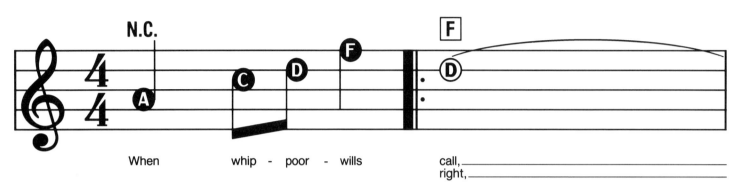

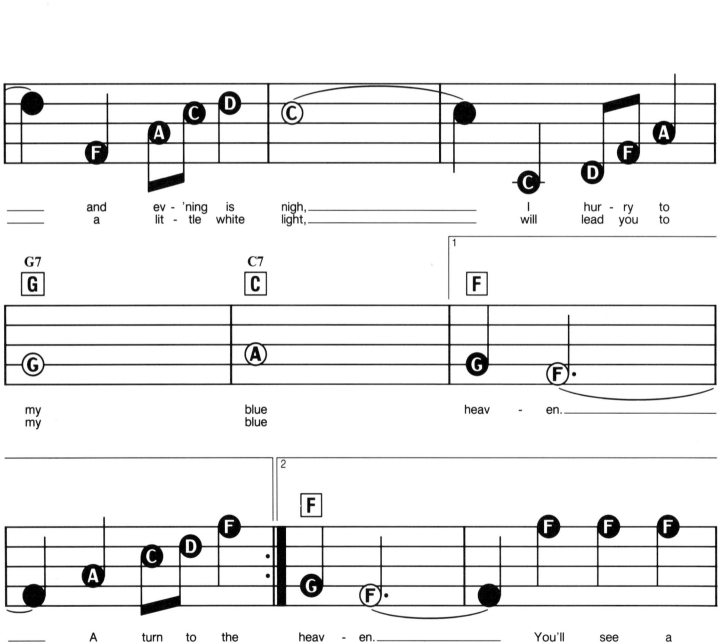

73

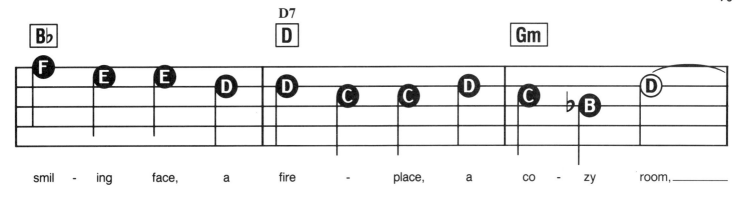

smil - ing face, a fire - place, a co - zy room, _____

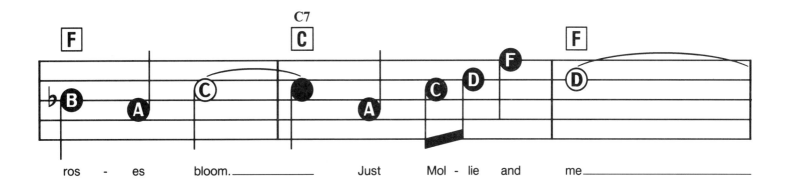

_____ a lit - tle nest that's nes - tled where the

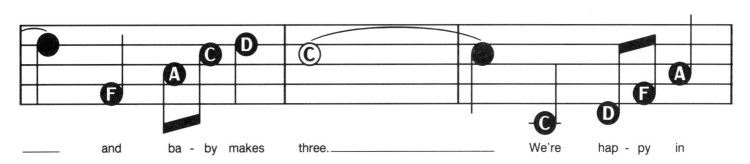

ros - es bloom. _____ Just Mol - lie and me _____

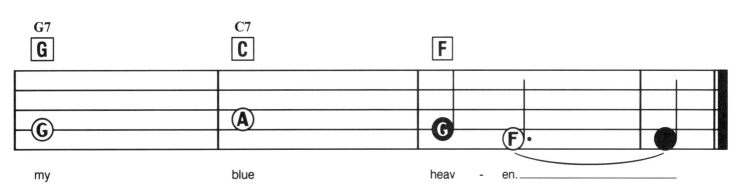

_____ and ba - by makes three. _____ We're hap - py in

my blue heav - en. _____

My Melody of Love

Registration 2
Rhythm: Polka or March

English and Polish Lyrics by Bobby Vinton
German Lyrics by George Buschor
Music by Henry Mayer

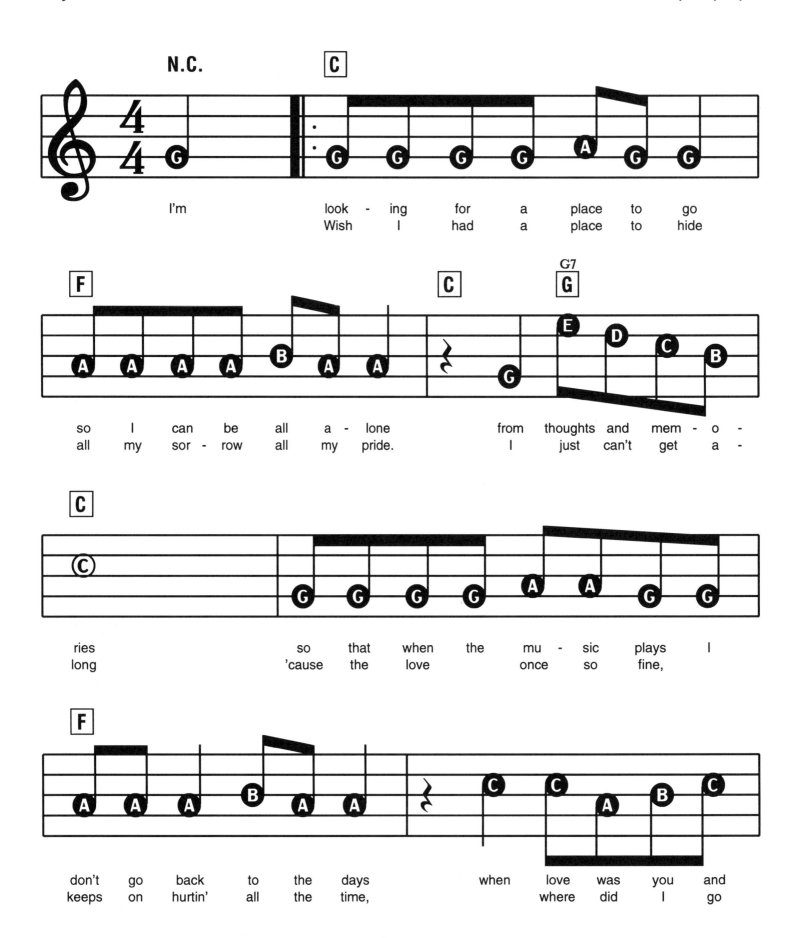

N.C.   C

I'm   look - ing   for   a   place   to   go
Wish   I   had   a   place   to   hide

F   C   G7 / G

so   I   can   be   all   a - lone   from   thoughts   and   mem - o -
all   my   sor - row   all   my   pride.   I   just   can't   get   a -

C

ries   so   that   when   the   mu - sic   plays   I
long   'cause   the   love   once   so   fine,

F

don't   go   back   to   the   days   when   love   was   you   and
keeps   on   hurtin'   all   the   time,   where   did   I   go

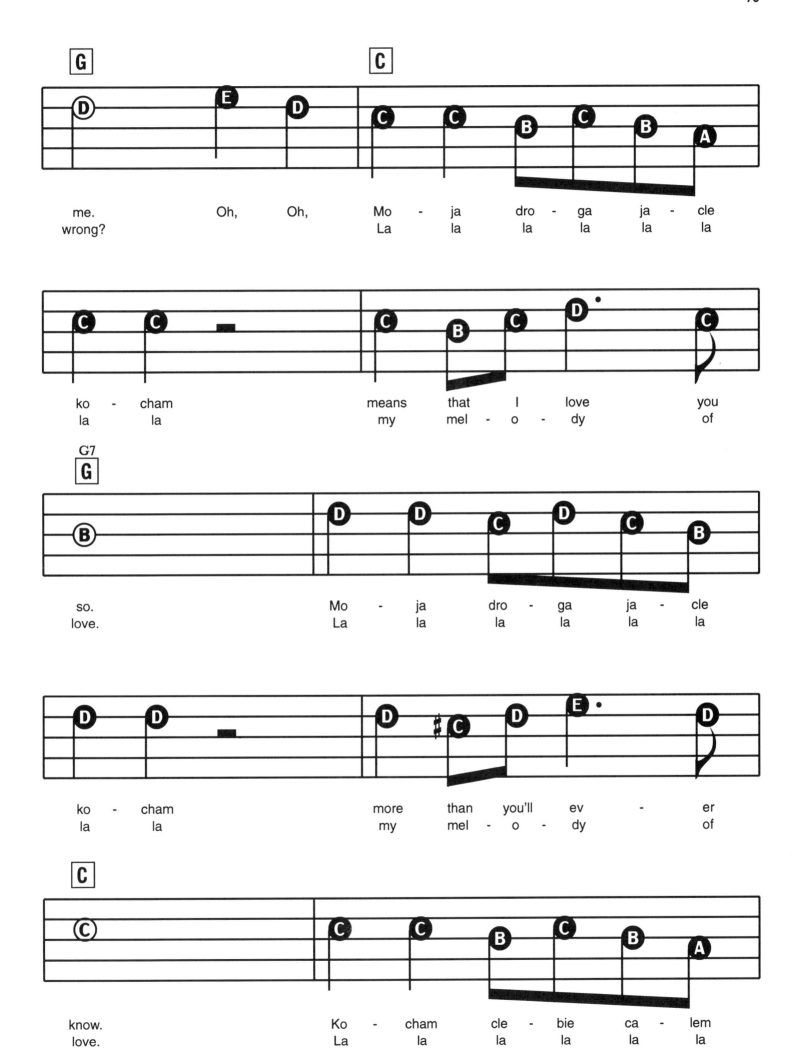

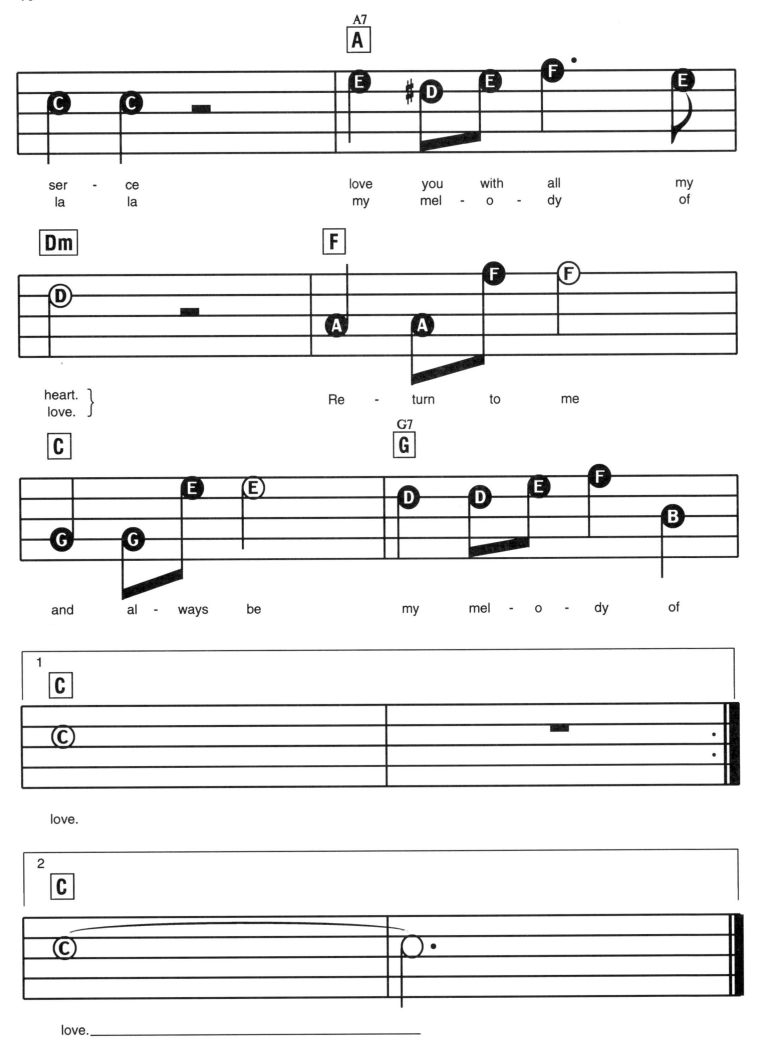

ser - ce   love you with all my
la la   my mel - o - dy of

heart. }
love. }

Re - turn to me

and al - ways be my mel - o - dy of

1

love.

2

love._____

One Dozen Roses

Registration 9
Rhythm: Fox Trot or Swing

Words by Roger Lewis and "Country" Joe Washburn
Music by Dick Jurgens and Walter Donovan

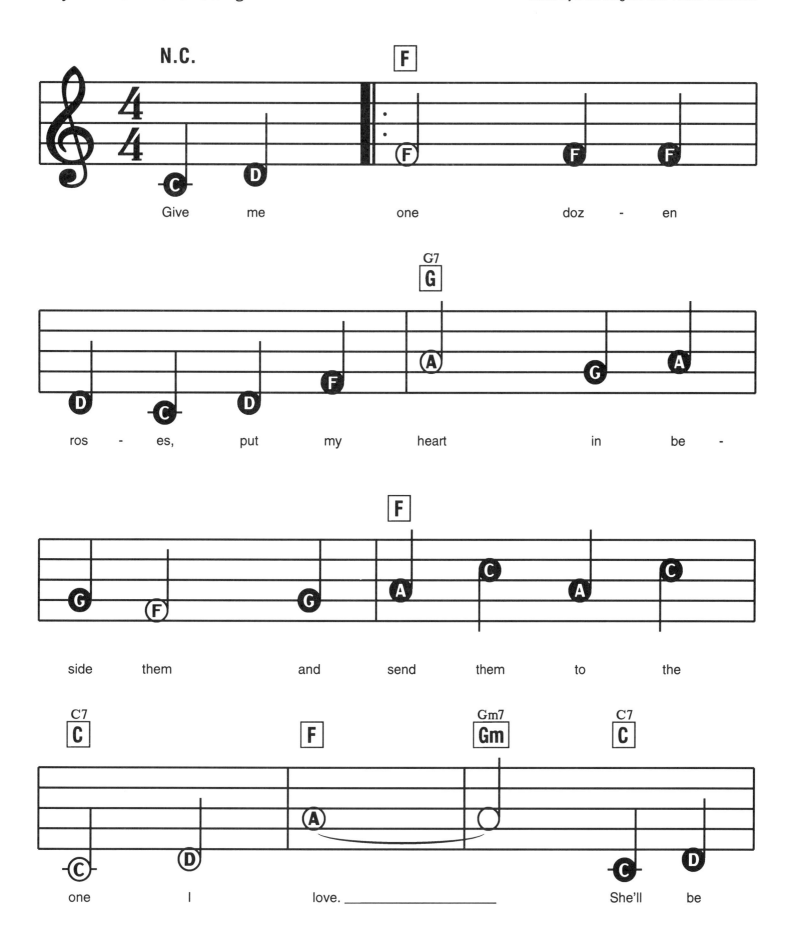

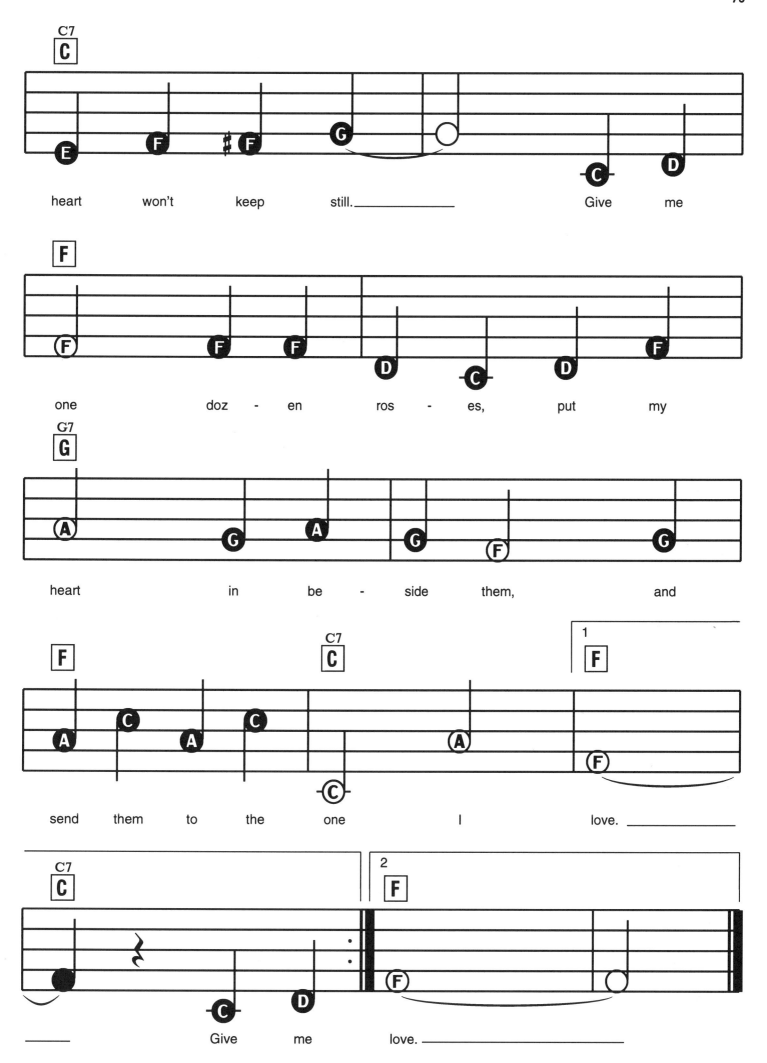

Oh! You Beautiful Doll

Registration 3
Rhythm: Fox Trot or Swing

Words by A. Seymour Brown
Music by Nat D. Ayer

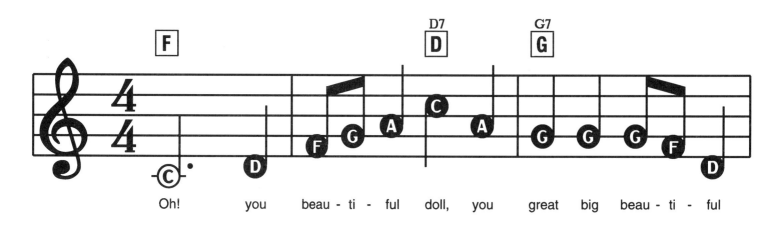

Oh! you beau - ti - ful doll, you great big beau - ti - ful

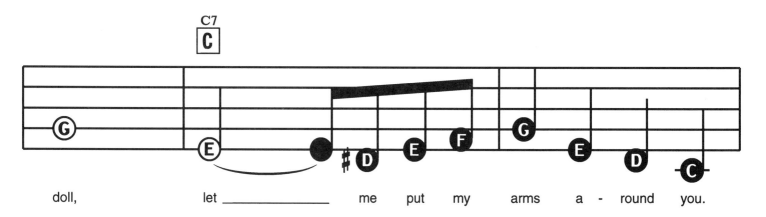

doll, let _____ me put my arms a - round you.

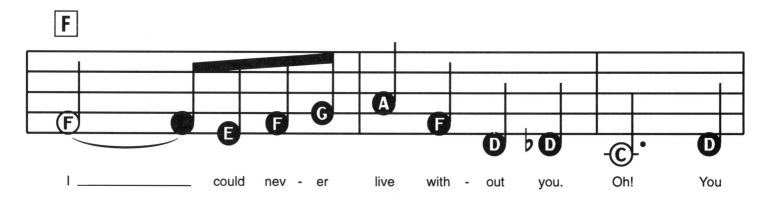

I _____ could nev - er live with - out you. Oh! You

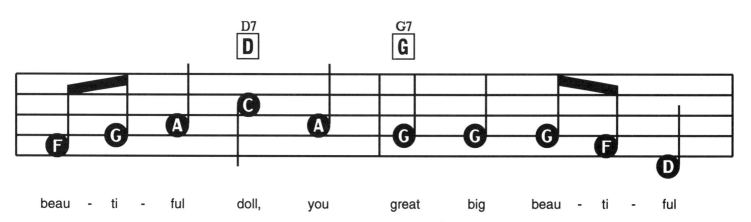

beau - ti - ful doll, you great big beau - ti - ful

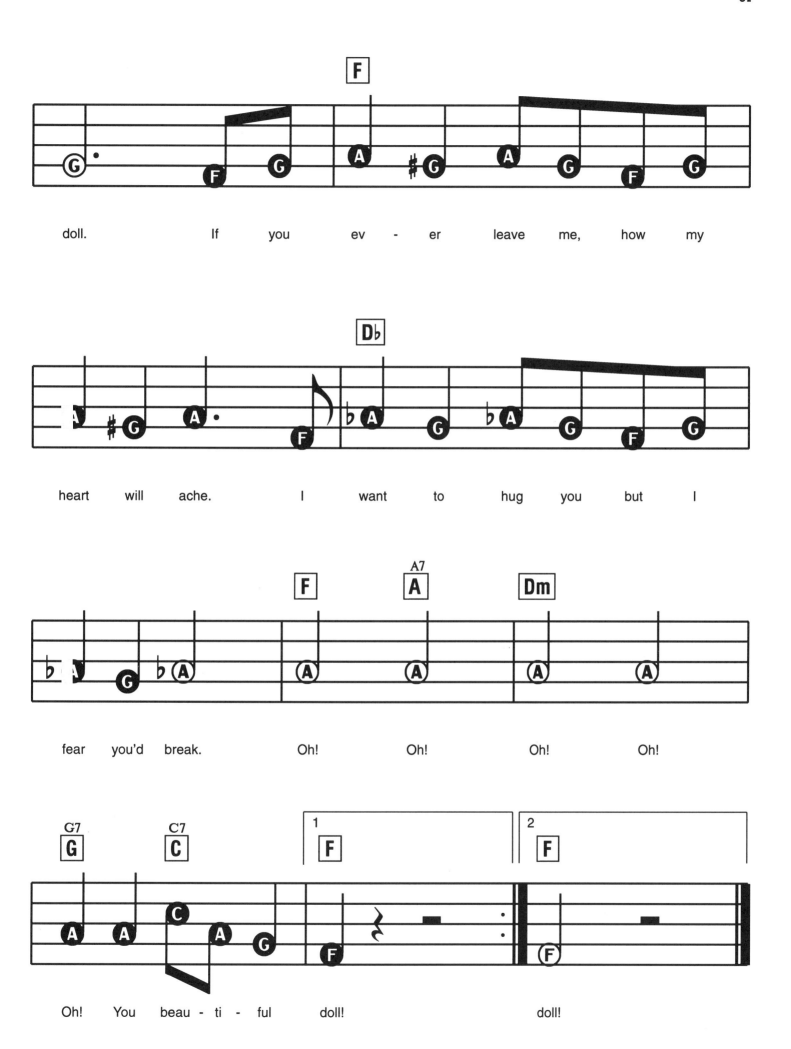

The Old Fashioned Way
(Les Plaisirs Demodes)

English Words by Al Kasha and Joel Hirschhorn
Original Words by Charles Aznavour
Music by George Garvarentz

Registration 4
Rhythm: Ballad

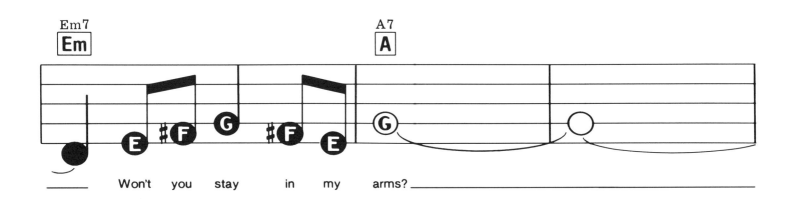

Dance _____ in the old fash - ioned way. _____

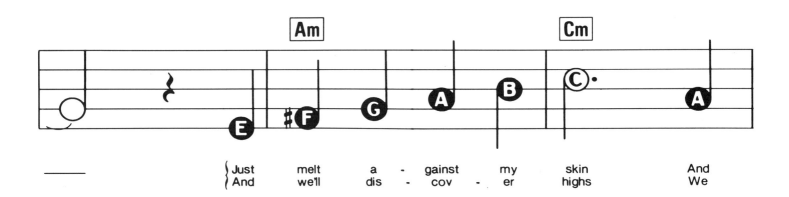

_____ Won't you stay in my arms? _____

Just melt a - gainst my skin And
And we'll dis - cov - er highs We

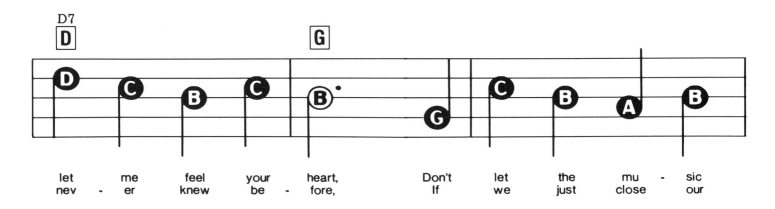

let me feel your heart, Don't let the mu - sic
nev - er knew be - fore, If we just close our

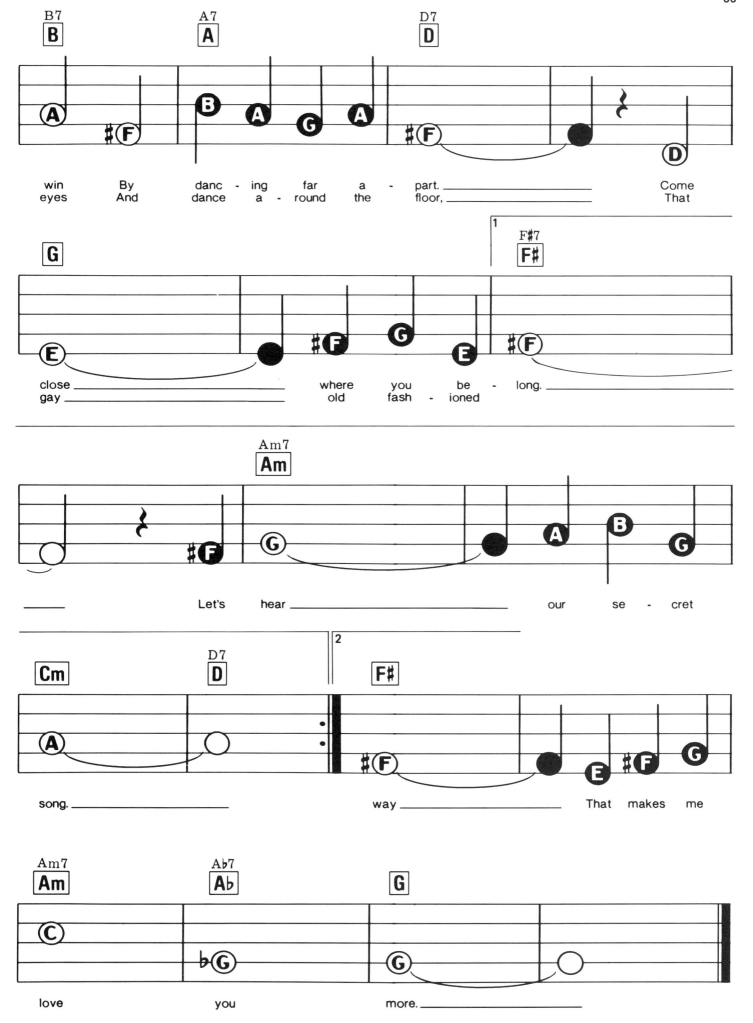

Red Sails in the Sunset

Registration 3
Rhythm: Fox Trot or Ballad

Words by Jimmy Kennedy
Music by Hugh Williams (Will Grosz)

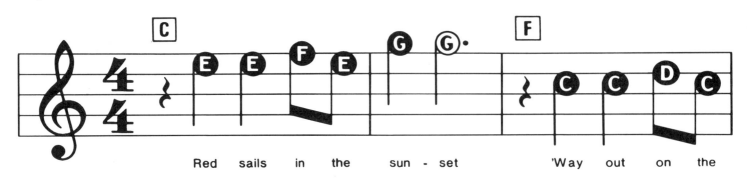

Red sails in the sun-set 'Way out on the

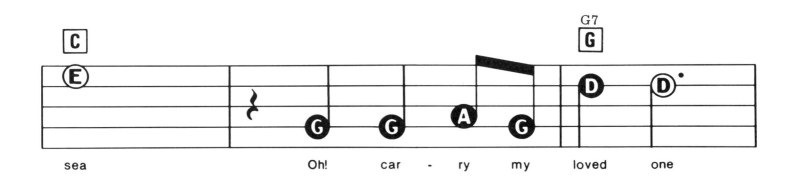

sea Oh! car-ry my loved one

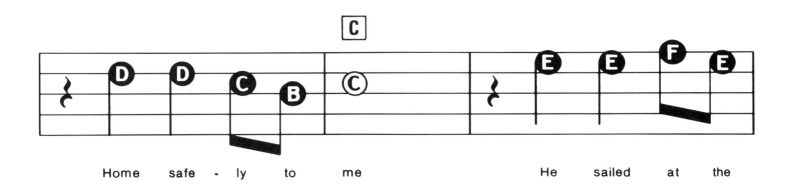

Home safe-ly to me He sailed at the

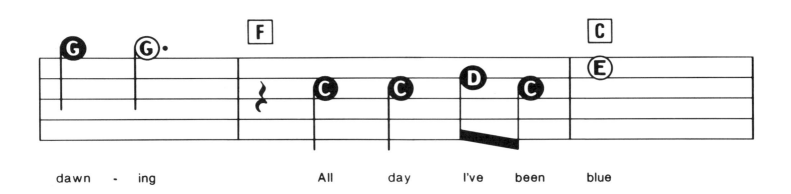

dawn-ing All day I've been blue

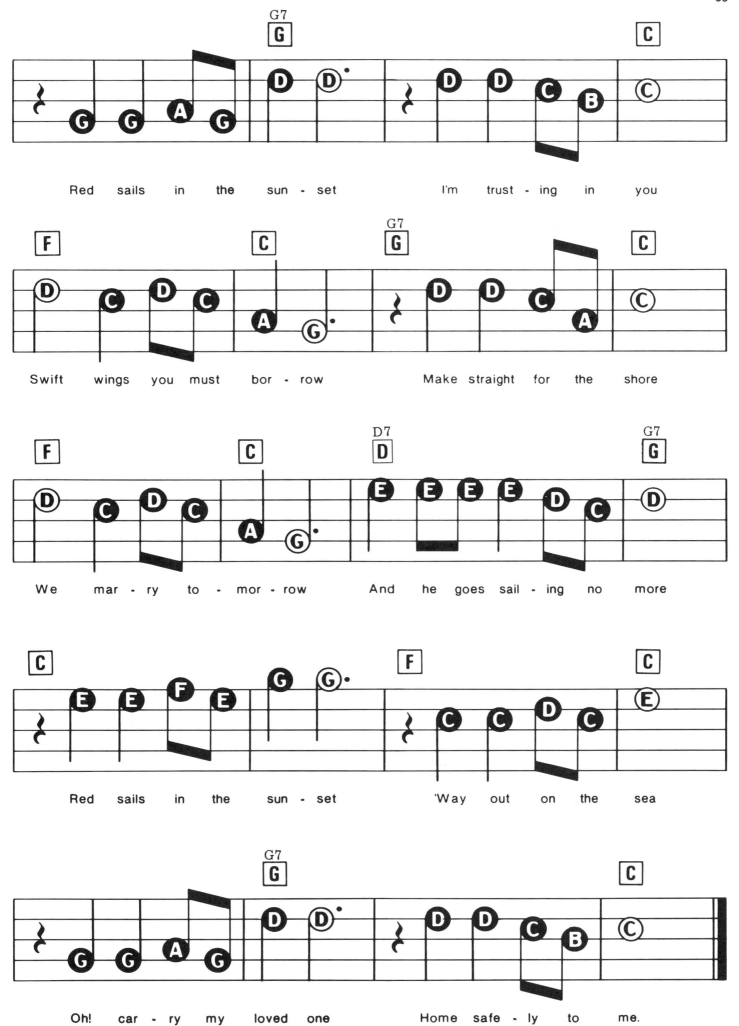

Side by Side

Registration 7
Rhythm: Fox Trot or Swing

Words and Music by
Harry Woods

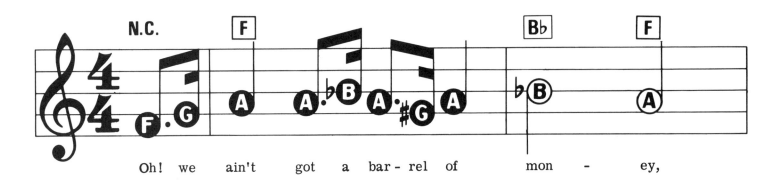

Oh! we ain't got a bar - rel of mon - ey,

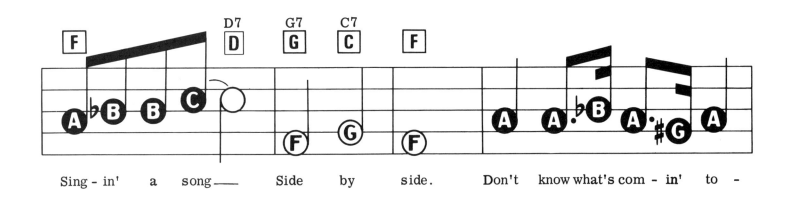

May - be we're rag - ged and fun - ny, But we'll trav - el a - long

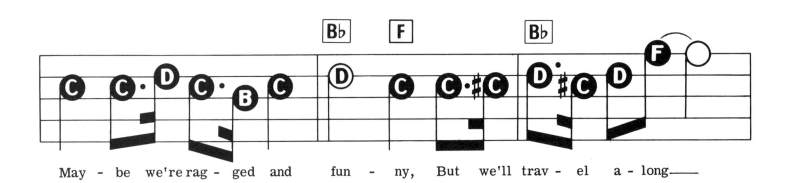

Sing - in' a song Side by side. Don't know what's com - in' to -

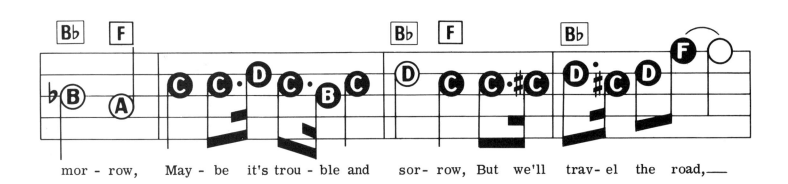

mor - row, May - be it's trou - ble and sor - row, But we'll trav - el the road,

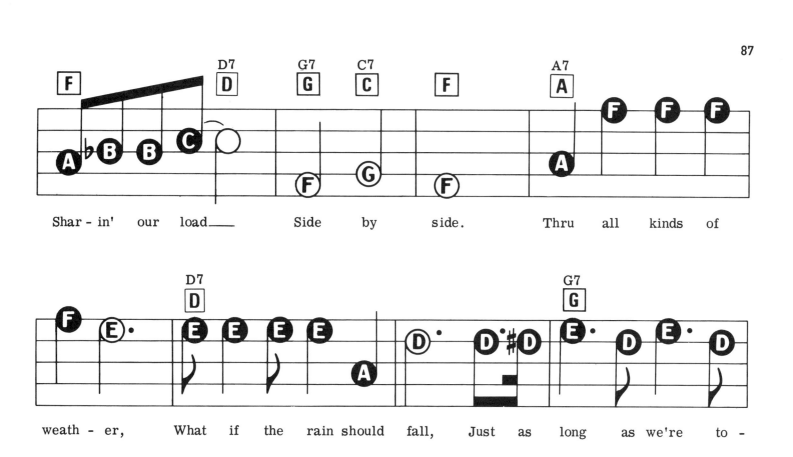

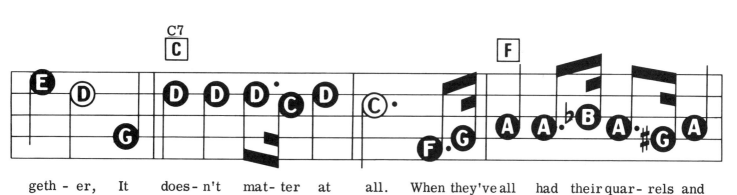

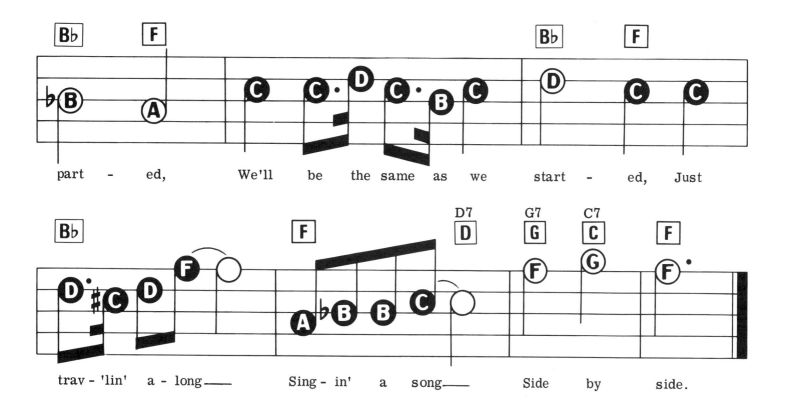

Soft Lights and Sweet Music
from the Stage Production FACE THE MUSIC

Registration 1
Rhythm: Fox Trot or Ballad

Words and Music by
Irving Berlin

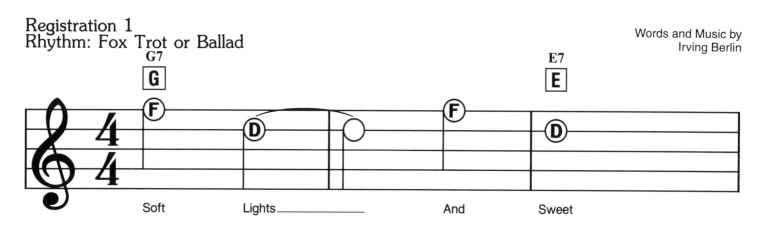

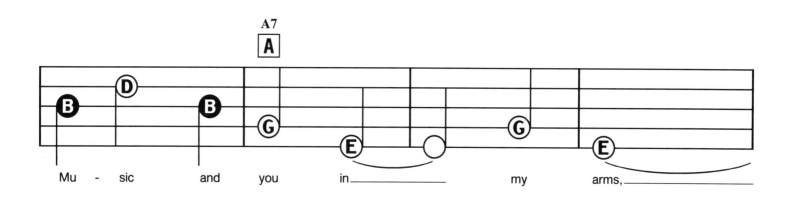

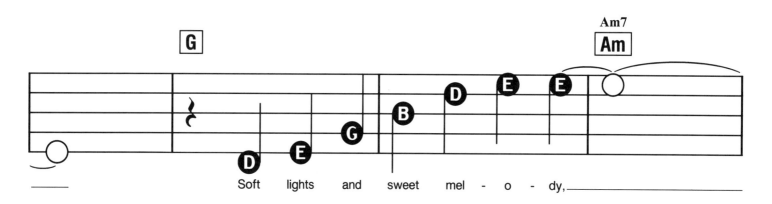

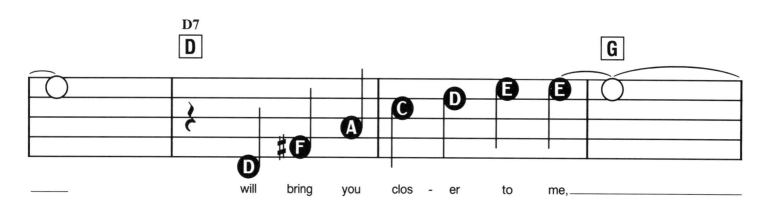

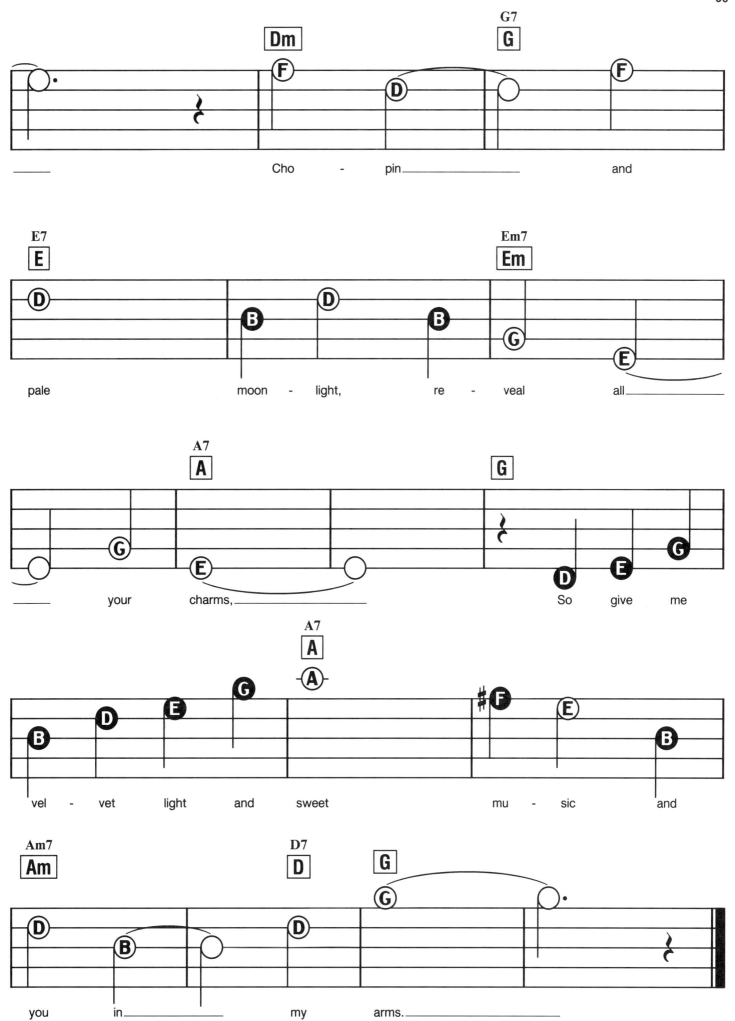

Somewhere, My Love
Lara's Theme from DOCTOR ZHIVAGO

Registration 9
Rhythm: Waltz

Lyric by Paul Francis Webster
Music by Maurice Jarre

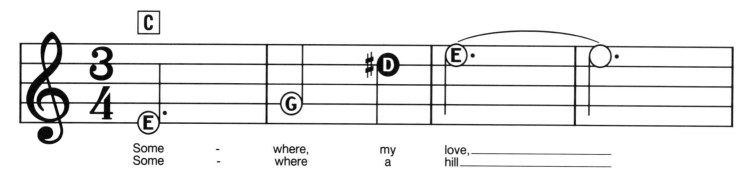

Some - where, my love,_____
Some - where a hill_____

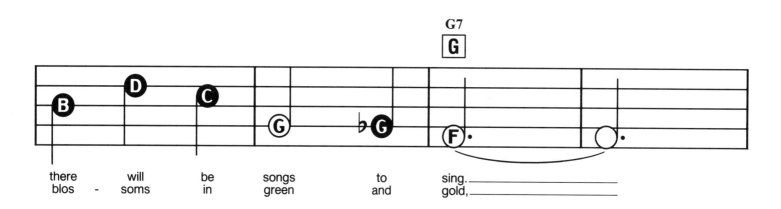

there will be songs to sing._____
blos - soms in green and gold,_____

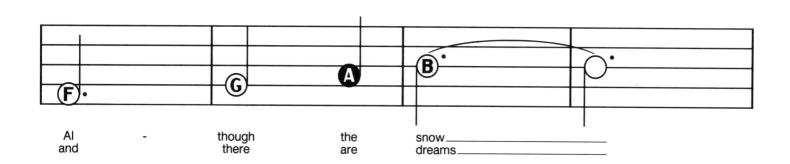

Al - though the snow_____
and there are dreams_____

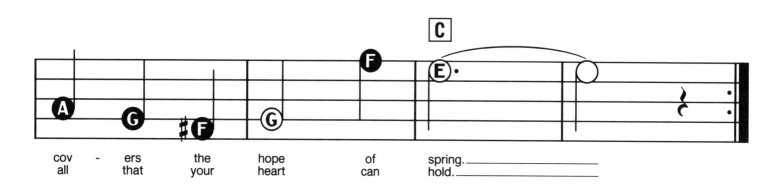

cov - ers the hope of spring._____
all that your heart can hold._____

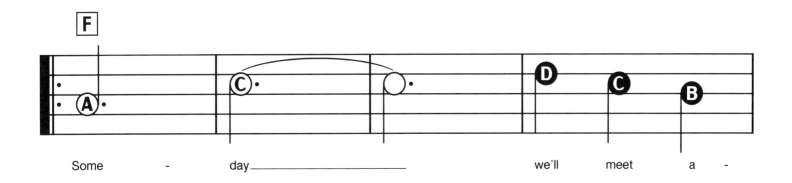

Some - day_____ we'll meet a -

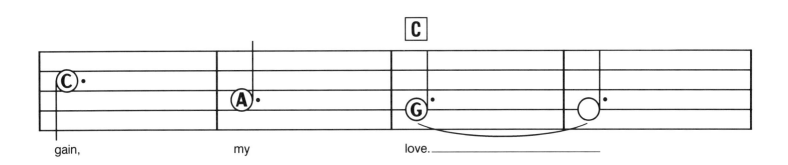

gain, my love._____

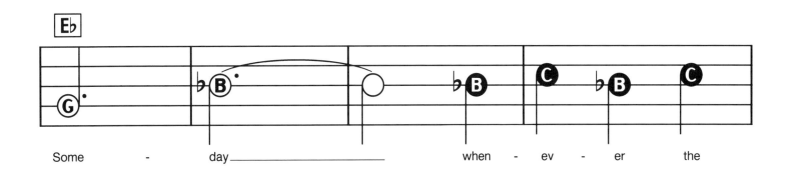

Some - day_____ when - ev - er the

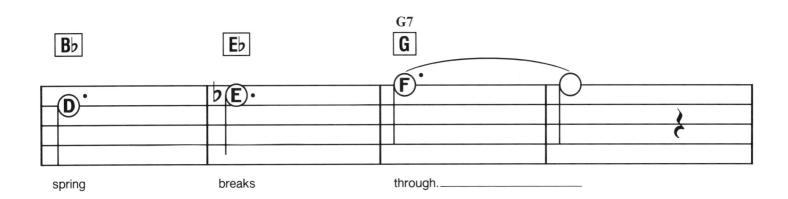

spring breaks through._____

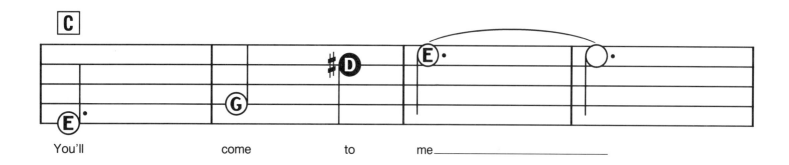

You'll   come   to   me

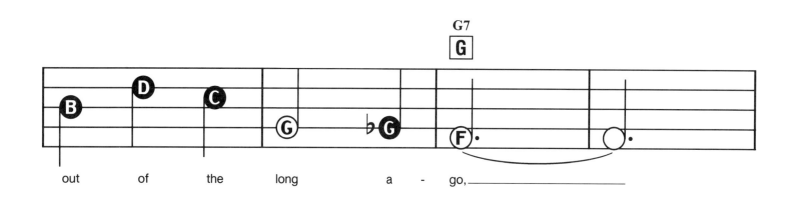

out   of   the   long   a - go,

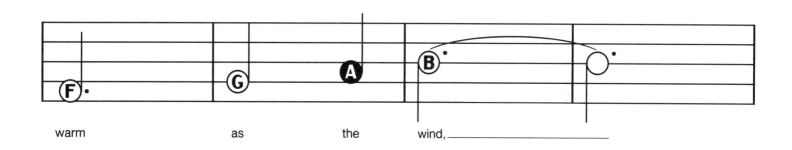

warm   as   the   wind,

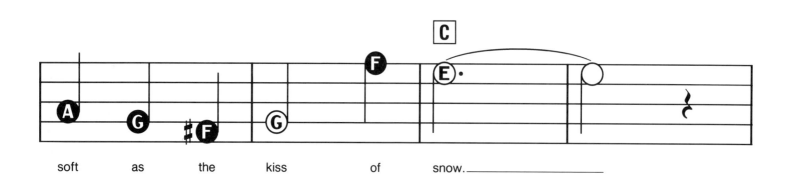

soft   as   the   kiss   of   snow.

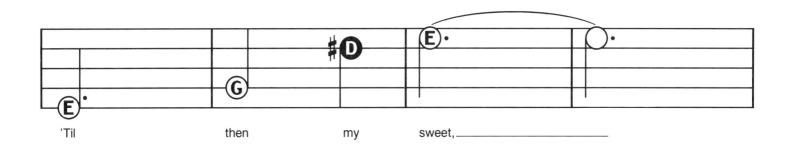

'Til then my sweet, _____

G7

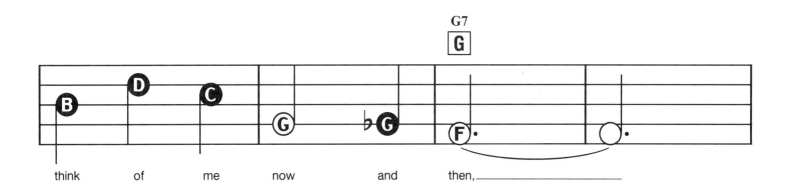

think of me now and then, _____

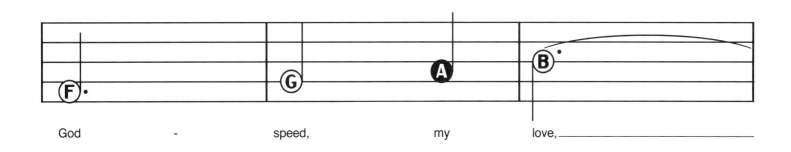

God - speed, my love, _____

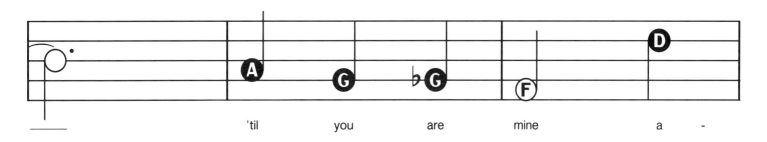

____ 'til you are mine a -

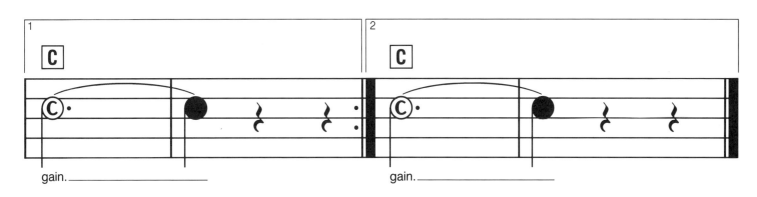

gain. _____   gain. _____

Spanish Eyes

Registration 3
Rhythm: Latin or Bossa Nova

Words by Charles Singleton and Eddie Snyder
Music by Bert Kaempfert

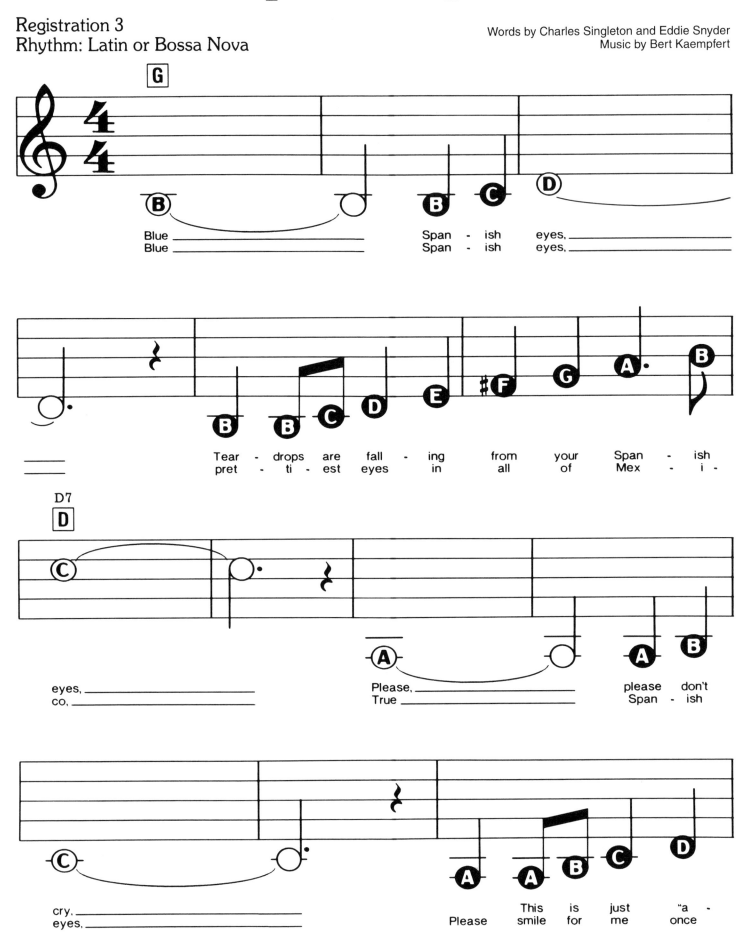

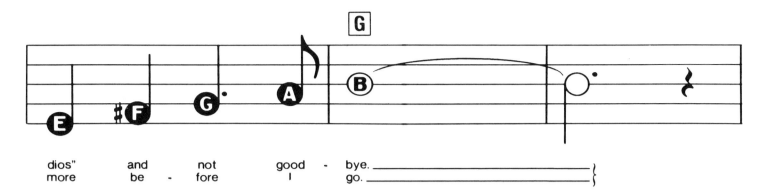

dios"   and   not   good - bye. _____
more   be - fore   I   go. _____

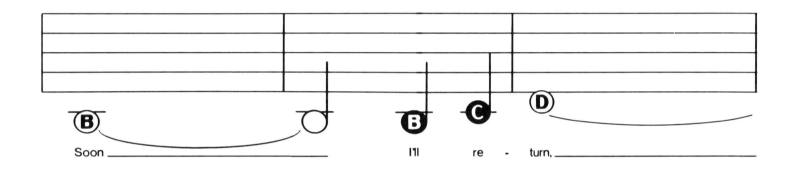

Soon _____ I'll   re - turn, _____

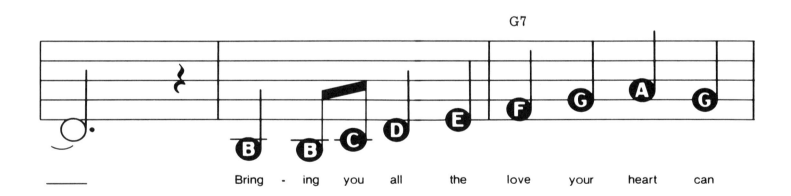

_____   Bring - ing   you   all   the   love   your   heart   can

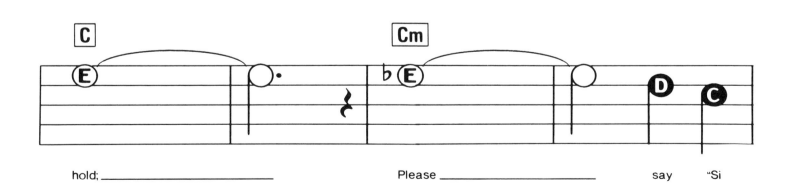

hold; _____   Please _____   say   "Si

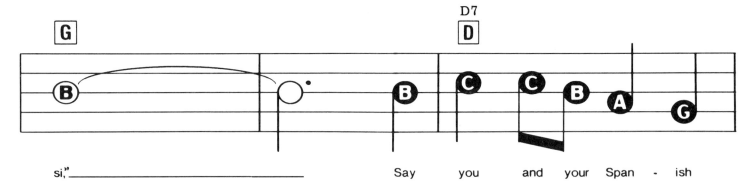

si,"_____ Say you and your Span - ish

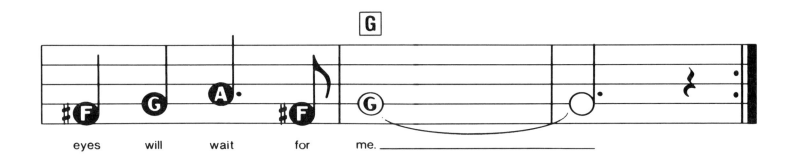

eyes will wait for me. _____

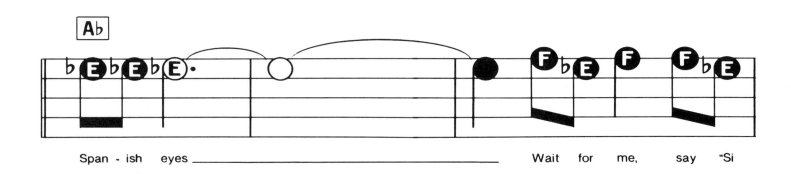

Span - ish eyes _____ Wait for me, say "Si

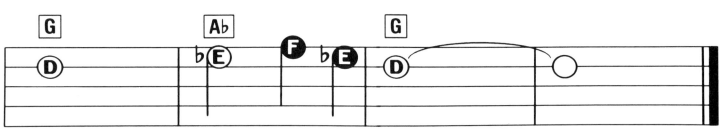

Si!" _____

You Made Me Love You
(I Didn't Want to Do It)
from BROADWAY MELODY OF 1938

Registration 7
Rhythm: Fox Trot

Words by Joe McCarthy
Music by James V. Monaco

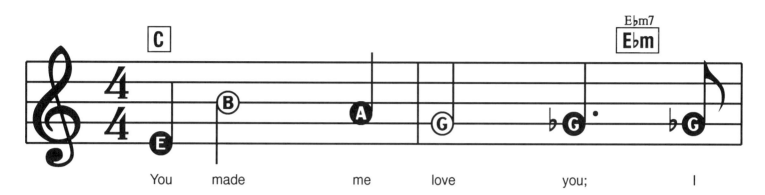

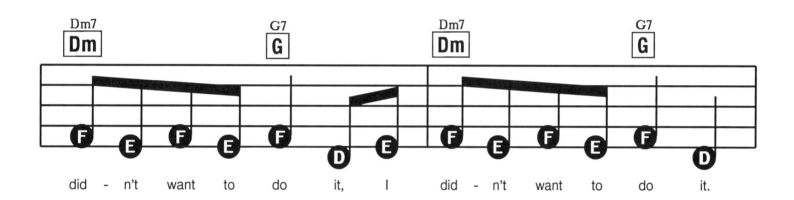

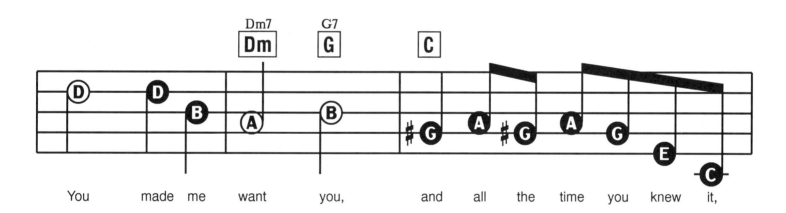

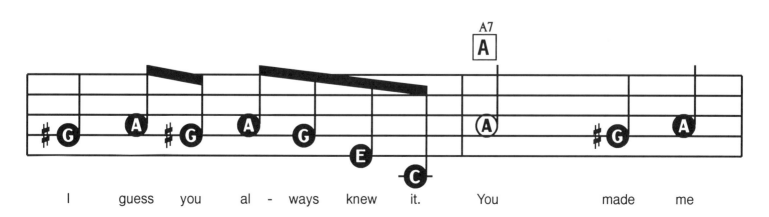

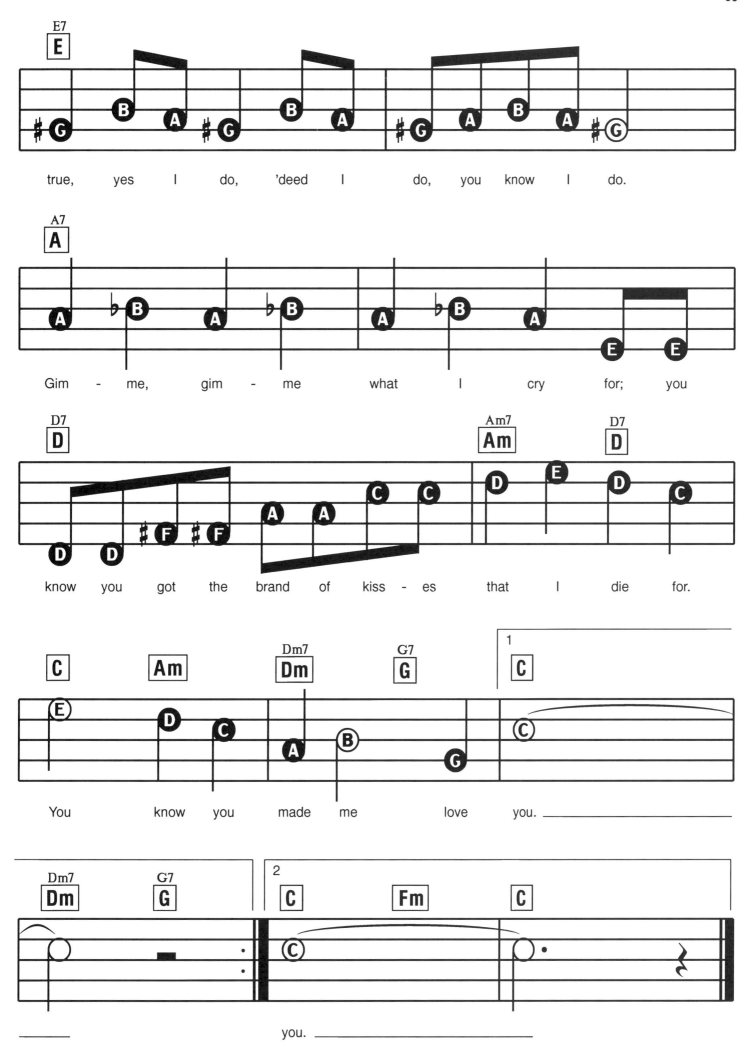

They Say It's Wonderful
from the Stage Production ANNIE GET YOUR GUN

Registration 10
Rhythm: Fox Trot or Ballad

Words and Music by
Irving Berlin

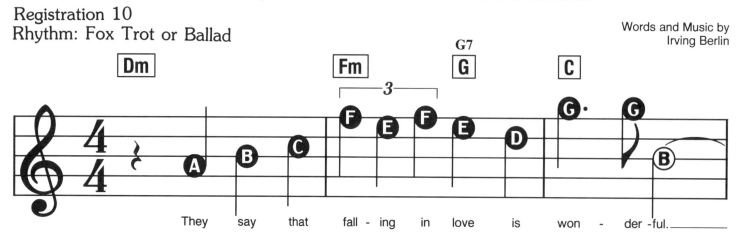

They say that fall - ing in love is won - der -ful.____

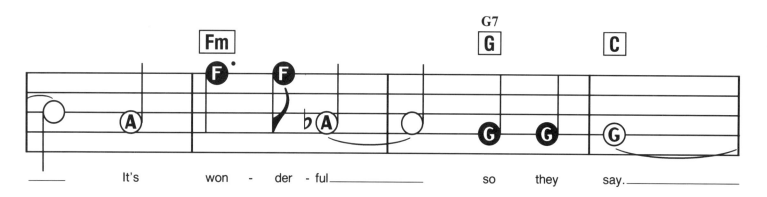

____ It's won - der -ful_____ so they say.____

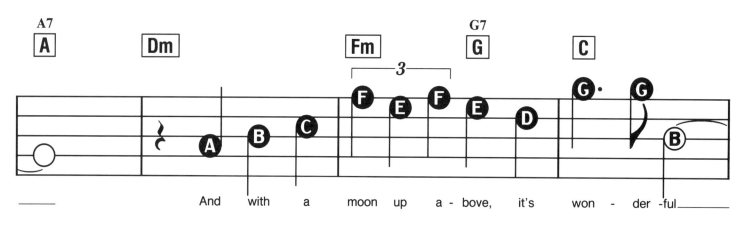

____ And with a moon up a - bove, it's won - der -ful

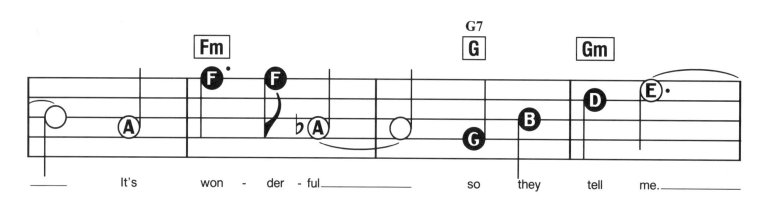

____ It's won - der -ful_____ so they tell me.

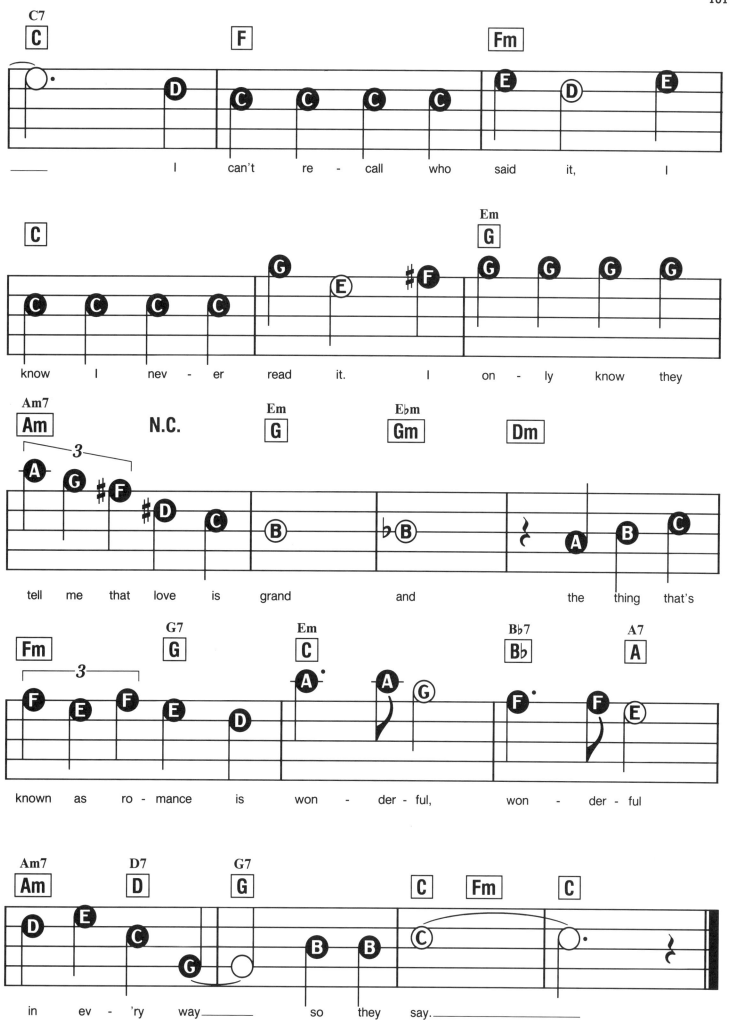

Till We Two Are One

Registration 4
Rhythm: Fox Trot or Ballad

Words by Tom Glazer
Music by Larry and Billy Martin

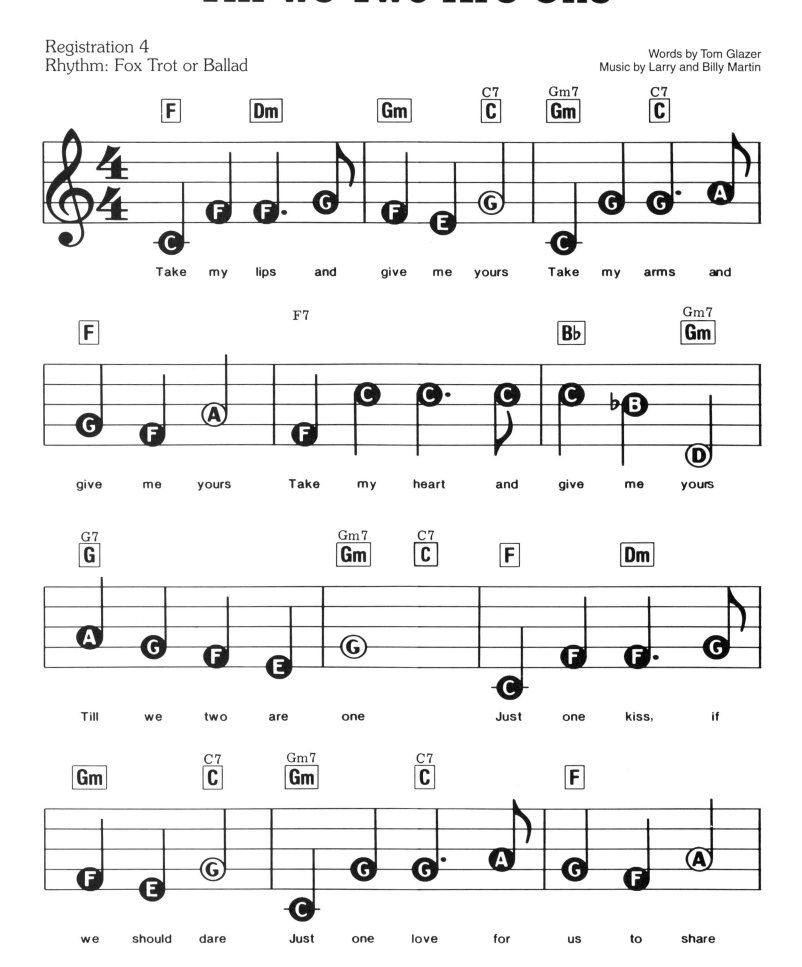

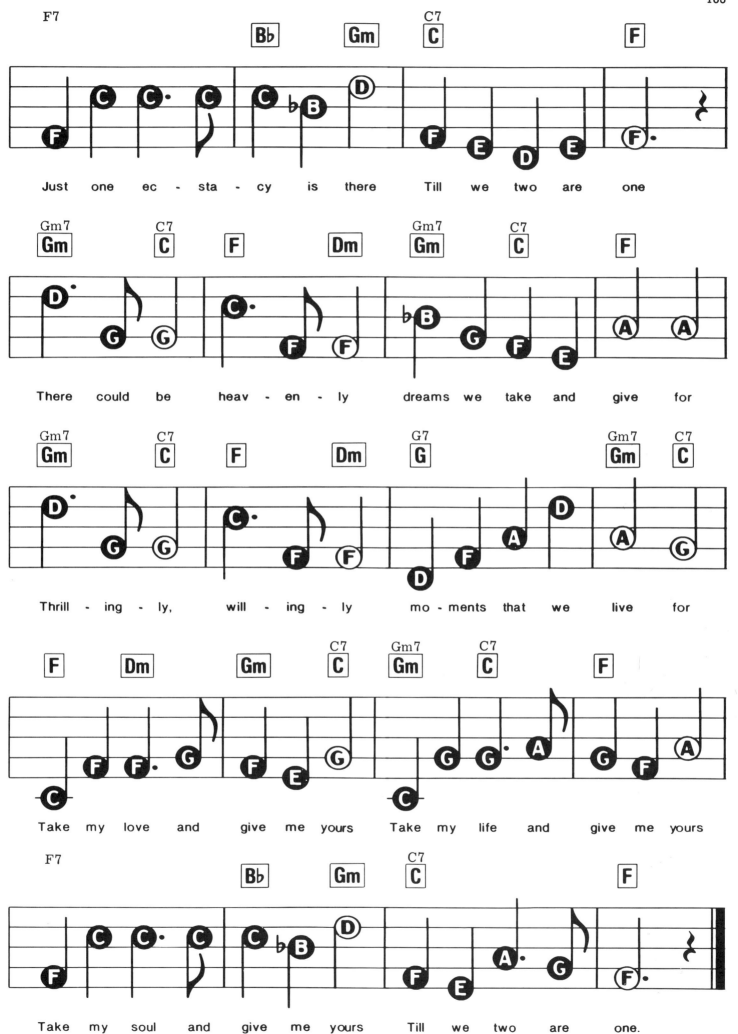

To Each His Own

from the Paramount Picture TO EACH HIS OWN
from the Paramount Picture THE CONVERSATION

Registration 2
Rhythm: Fox Trot or Swing

Words and Music by Jay Livingston
and Ray Evans

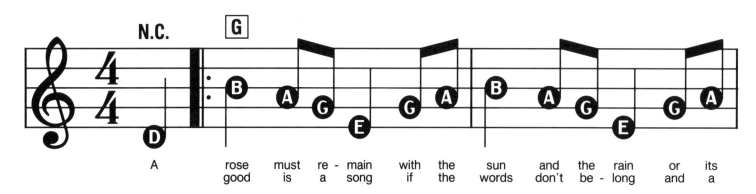

A
rose must re-main with the sun and the rain or its
good is a song if the sun words don't be-long and a

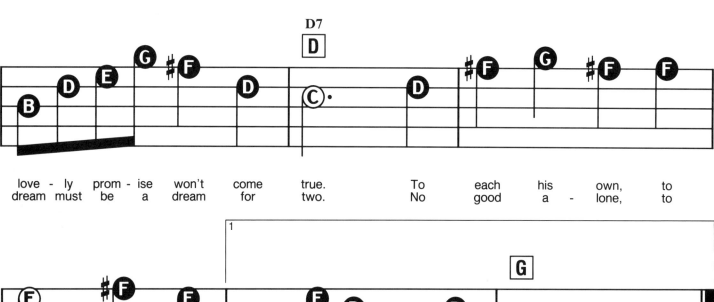

love-ly prom-ise won't come true. To each his own, to
dream must be a dream come for two. No each good a-lone, to

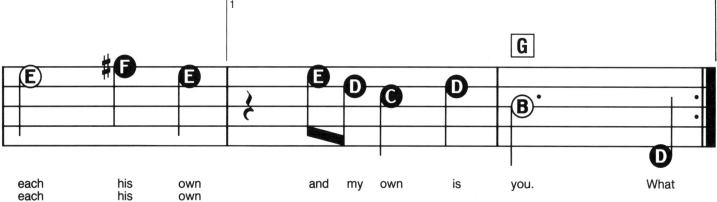

each his own and my own is you. What
each his own

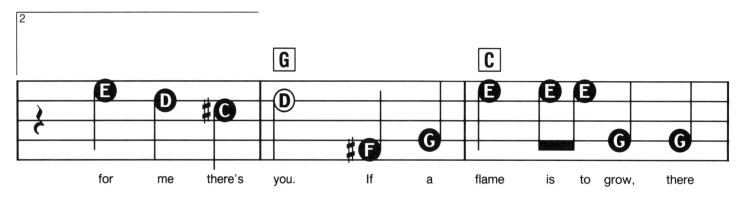

for me there's you. If a flame is to grow, there

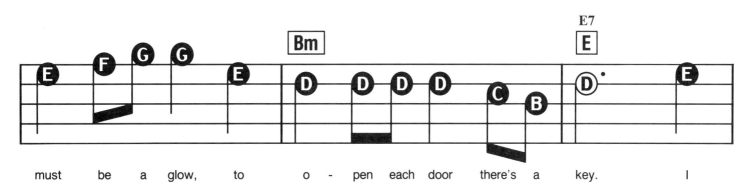

must be a glow, to o - pen each door there's a key. I

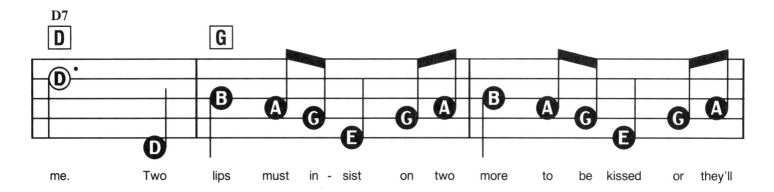

need you, I know, I can't let you go, your touch means too much to

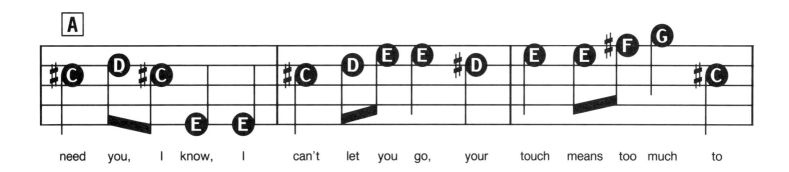

me. Two lips must in - sist on two more to be kissed or they'll

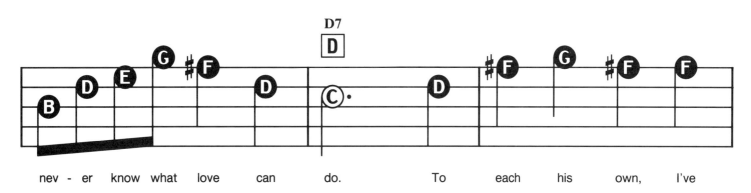

nev - er know what love can do. To each his own, I've

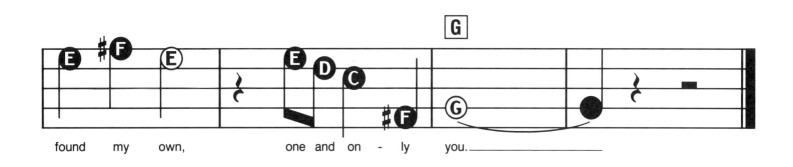

found my own, one and on - ly you._____

To Love Again
Theme from THE EDDY DUCHIN STORY

Registration 10
Rhythm: Waltz

Based on Chopin's E Flat Nocturne
Words by Ned Washington
Music by Morris Stoloff and George Sidney

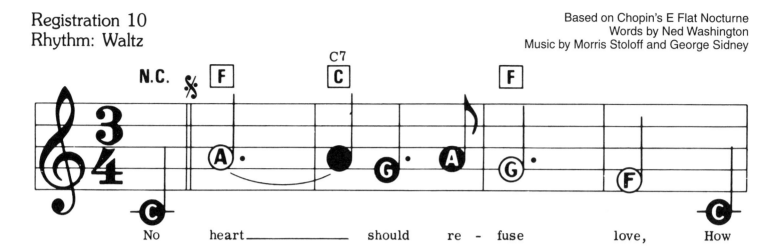

No heart _____ should re - fuse love, How

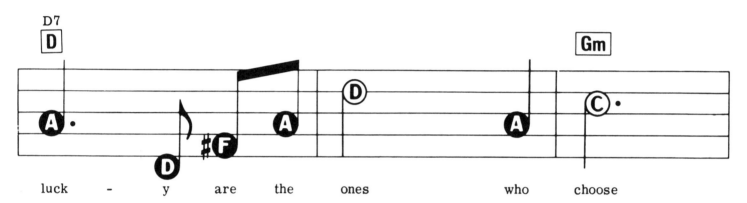

luck - y are the ones who choose

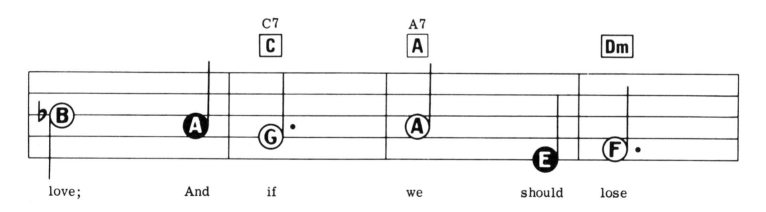

love; And if we should lose

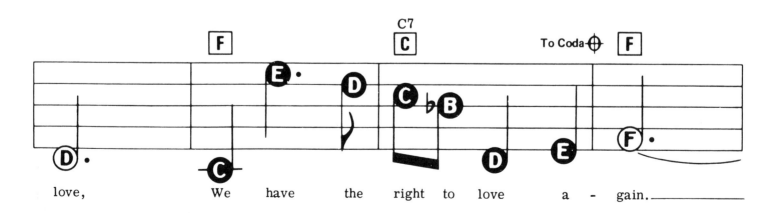

love, We have the right to love a - gain. _____

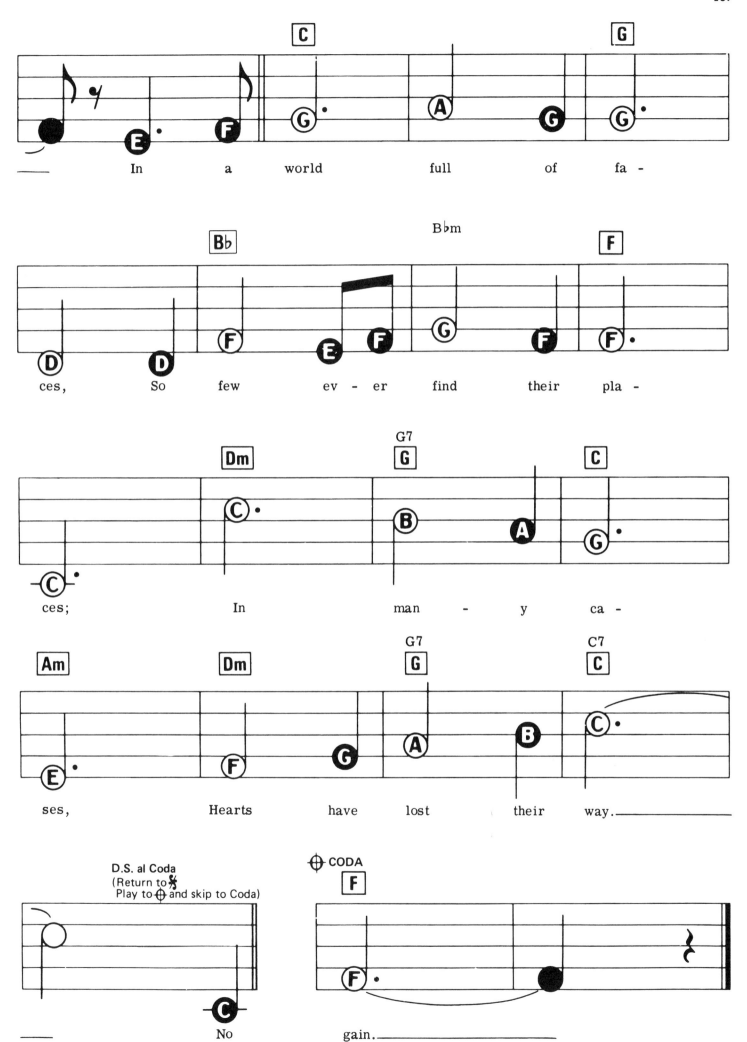

True Love
from HIGH SOCIETY

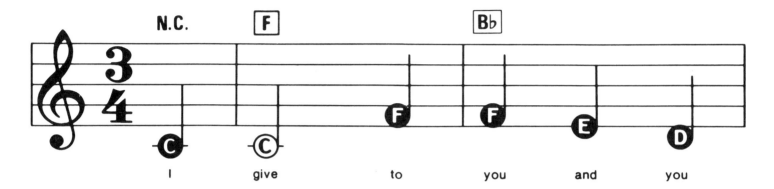

Registration 4
Rhythm: Waltz

Words and Music by
Cole Porter

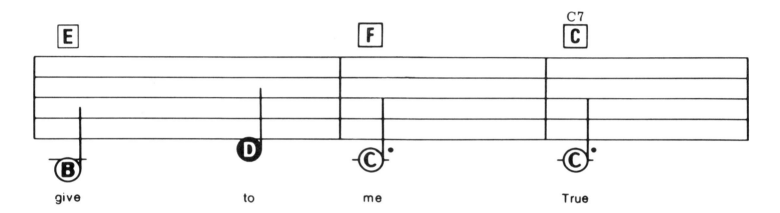

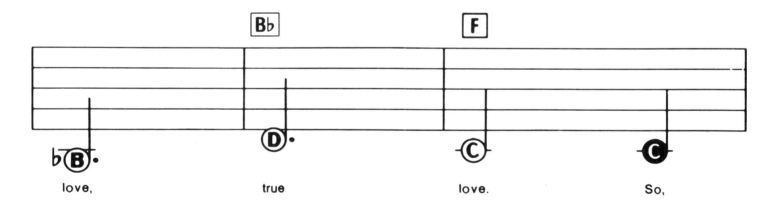

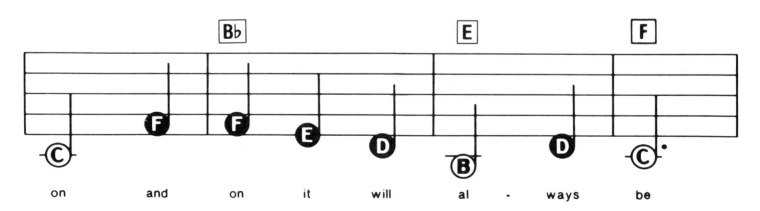

109

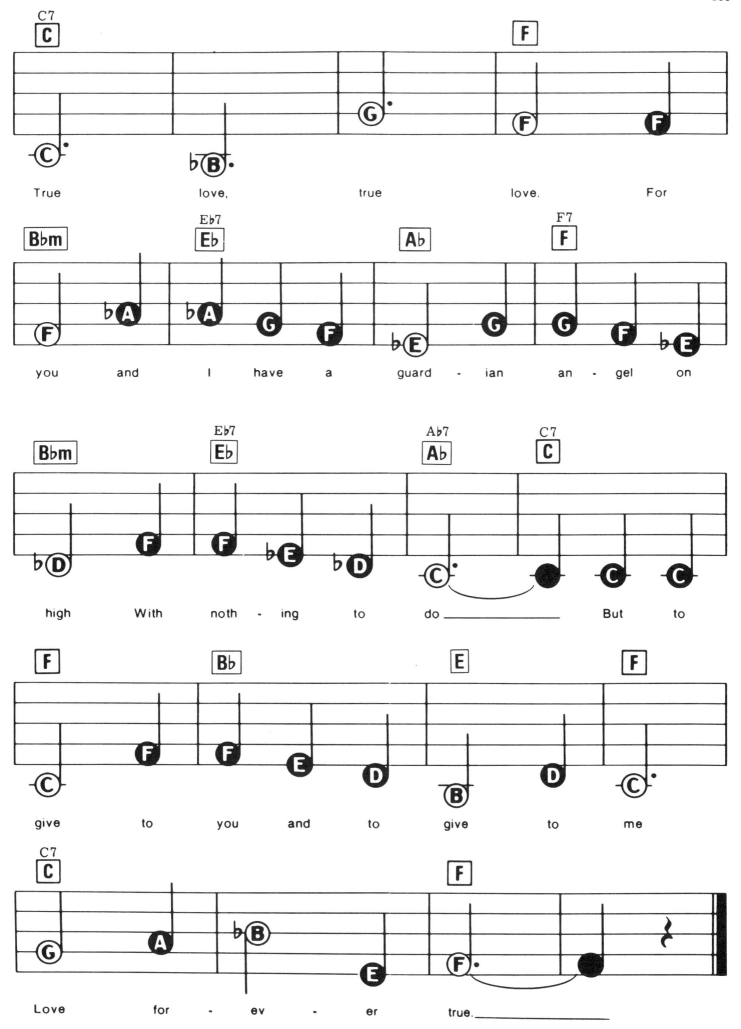

Yours
(Cuandao Se Quiere de Veras)

Registration 2
Rhythm: Rhumba or Latin

Words by Albert Gamse and Jack Sherr
Music by Gonzalo Roig

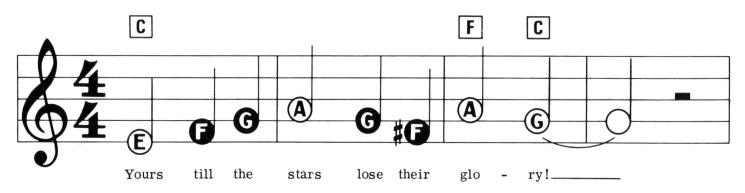

Yours till the stars lose their glo - ry!_____

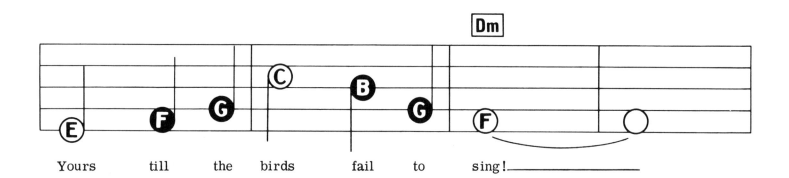

Yours till the birds fail to sing!_____

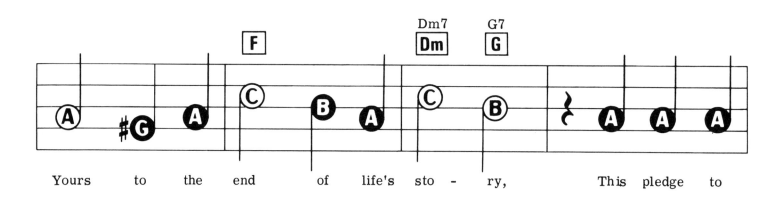

Yours to the end of life's sto - ry, This pledge to

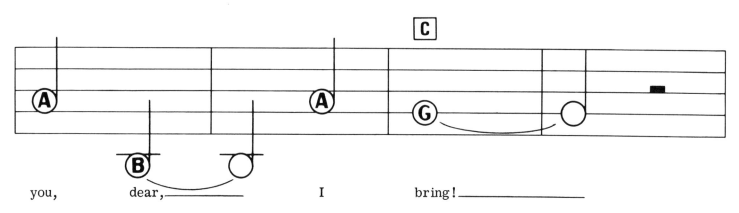

you, dear,_____ I bring!_____

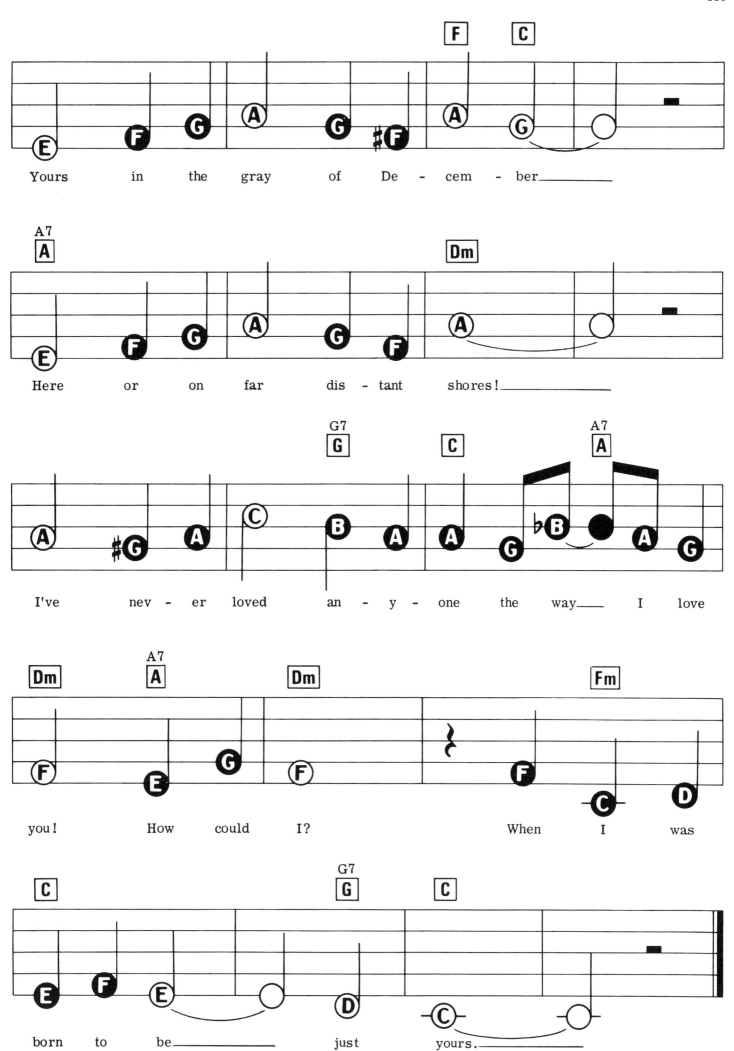

 **Registration Guide**

- Match the Registration number on the song to the corresponding numbered category below. Select and activate an instrumental sound available on your instrument.

- Choose an automatic rhythm appropriate to the mood and style of the song. (Consult your Owner's Guide for proper operation of automatic rhythm features.)

- Adjust the tempo and volume controls to comfortable settings.

Registration

1	Flute, Pan Flute, Jazz Flute
2	Clarinet, Organ
3	Violin, Strings
4	Brass, Trumpet
5	Synth Ensemble, Accordion, Brass
6	Pipe Organ, Harpsichord
7	Jazz Organ, Vibraphone, Vibes, Electric Piano, Jazz Guitar
8	Piano, Electric Piano
9	Trumpet, Trombone, Clarinet, Saxophone, Oboe
10	Violin, Cello, Strings